THE LAX FAMILY EDITION

TZURBA
M'RABANAN
לעילוי נשמת מאיר (מישו) אלימלך ז"ל

TZURBA M'RABANAN

WITH ENGLISH TRANSLATION, COMMENTARY AND ESSAYS

A concise learning method from the Talmudic source
through modern-day halachic application

Selected Laws of Pesach

SELWYN & ROS SMITH AND FAMILY

MIZRACHI

תנועת תורנית

Torah
Leadership

IN PARTNERSHIP WITH
ERETZ HEMDAH AND WORLD MIZRACHI

ארץ
חמדה

ERETZ HEMDAH
Institute for Advanced Jewish Studies
Jerusalem

Tzurba M'Rabanan
First English Edition, 2022
Selected Laws of Pesach, March 2022

Excerpts from *Tzurba* Volumes 1 (Second English Edition) and 5 (First English Edition)

Mizrachi Press
54 King George Street, PO Box 7720
Jerusalem, 9107602, Israel
www.mizrachi.org

Distributors: World Tzurba Institute   Shikey Press
                 896 Central Avenue   Cambridge, MA
                 Woodmere, NY 11598   www.ShikeyPress.com

ISBN: 979-8-9858054-7-5

Written and compiled by Rav Benzion Algazi
Translation and Authors of 'Additions of the English Editors': Rav Eli Ozarowski and Rav Doron Podlashuk

Proofreader: Rav Yaakov Felder (Volume 5)

Essays by *Selwyn & Ros Smith and Family – Manhigut Toranit* participants and graduates:
Rav Otniel Fendel, Rav Joel Kenigsberg

Director, Manhigut Toranit: Rav Doron Podlashuk
General Editor: Rav Eli Ozarowski

Creative Director: Jonny Lipczer
Design and Typesetting: Daniel Safran

With thanks to Sefaria for some of the English translations, including those from the William Davidson
digital edition of the Koren Noé Talmud, with commentary by Rabbi Adin Even-Israel Steinsaltz.

Feedback is welcome: comments@mizrachi.org

www.tzurba.com
www.tzurbaolami.com

TZURBA M'RABANAN

EXCERPTS FROM
VOLUME 1
THE KUPFERBERG AND UCKO FAMILIES VOLUME
AND VOLUME 5
THE LAX FAMILY VOLUME

THE LAX FAMILY EDITION
IS DEDICATED
IN LOVING MEMORY
OF OUR DEAR SONS AND BROTHERS

Jonathan Theodore Lax z"l
Ethan James Lax z"l

לעילוי נשמת

יונתן טוביה בן מרדכי ז"ל
איתן אליעזר בן מרדכי ז"ל

ת.נ.צ.ב.ה.

MARSHA AND MICHAEL LAX
AMANDA AND AKIVA BLUMENTHAL
REBECCA AND RAMI LAIFER

CONTENTS

1

The Laws of Bedikat, Bitul and Bi'ur Chametz
הלכות בדיקת, ביטול וביעור חמץ

For quick reference, some long website URLs have been shortened.
For the complete list of referenced websites visit www.tzurbaolami.com.

ת	**Tanach**	
ת	**Talmud (Chazal)**	
ר	*Rishonim*	
א	*Acharonim*	
פ	**Contemporary Halachic Sources**	

STUDYING THE LAWS OF PESACH

The holiday of Pesach contains numerous relevant halachot with which a person must familiarize oneself, spanning from the laws of removing *chametz* from one's home, *kashering* one's kitchen, and baking matza, to performing the Pesach *seder* and all of the customs such as *kitniyot* that accompany the observance of the holiday. Therefore, it behooves a person to set aside time to study these halachot. In this *shiur*, we will study primarily the halachot of *bedikat chametz* (searching for *chametz*), *bitul chametz* (nullifying the *chametz*) and *bi'ur chametz* (burning the *chametz*), but we will begin with a short section on the importance of learning the laws of Pesach beforehand.

The **Gemara** in *Pesachim* records a rule that one should study the halachot of Pesach beginning thirty days prior to the holiday and uses it to derive one of the important halachot concerning *bedikat chametz*.

ח | Masechet Pesachim 6a

And Rav Yehuda said that **Rav said:** With regard to **one who sets sail, or one who departs in a caravan** traveling to a distant place; if he did so **before** it was **thirty days** prior to Passover, he **need not remove** the leaven from his possession. If he departs **within thirty days** of the Festival, **he must remove** the leaven... **What is the purpose of this** period of **thirty days** that renders it significant? **As it was taught** in a *baraita*: **One asks** about **and expound** upon **the halachot of Passover thirty days before Passover...**

The Gemara explains that this halacha is derived from the fact **that Moshe was standing at** the time of the **first** *Pesach*, on the fourteenth of Nissan, **and warning** the people **about** the halachot of **the second** *Pesach*, which occurred a month later, on the fourteenth of Iyar. **As it is stated** that God said to Moshe: **"Let the children of Israel perform the *Pesach* at its appointed time"** (*Bamidbar* 9:2). A subsequent verse says: "And Moshe told the children of Israel to perform the *Pesach*, and they performed the *Pesach* in the first month on the fourteenth of the month in the evening, in the desert of Sinai" (*Bamidbar* 9:4–5). **And it is written** in the next verse: **"And there were people who were impure due to a dead body** and could not perform the Passover on that day, and they came before Moshe and before Aharon on that day" (*Bamidbar* 9:6), at which point Moshe explained the halachot of the second *Pesach* to them. This proves that one begins studying the halachot of the Festival thirty days beforehand.

1. מסכת פסחים ו.

אמר רב יהודה, אמר רב: המפרש והיוצא בשיירא, קודם שלושים יום – אין זקוק לבער, תוך שלושים יום – זקוק לבער... הני שלושים יום מאי עבידתייהו? כדתניא: שואלין ודורשין בהלכות הפסח קודם הפסח שלושים יום...

שהרי משה עומד בפסח ראשון ומזהיר על הפסח שני, שנאמר: "וְיַעֲשׂוּ בְנֵי יִשְׂרָאֵל אֶת הַפָּסַח בְּמוֹעֲדוֹ" (במדבר ט, ב), וכתיב: "וַיְהִי אֲנָשִׁים אֲשֶׁר הָיוּ טְמֵאִים לְנֶפֶשׁ אָדָם" (שם, ו).

According to the Gemara, the fact that Moshe instructed individuals who were impure about the directive to observe *Pesach Sheini* when it was still the first day of Pesach indicates that one must discuss the halachot of Pesach thirty days beforehand. Many *Rishonim* raise a difficulty though that the **Gemara** in *Megilla* mentions an enactment of Moshe that the Jewish people should study the halachot of each holiday on the holiday itself, but makes no mention of doing so thirty days beforehand.

㊅ Masechet Megilla 4a

Moshe enacted for the Jewish people that they should ask questions about **and expound upon the subject of the day:** They should occupy themselves with **the halachot of Pesach on Pesach,** with **the halachot of Shavuot on Shavuot,** and with **the halachot of the festival** of Sukkot **on the festival** of Sukkot.

2. מסכת מגילה ד.

משה תיקן להם לישראל, שיהו שואלין ודורשין בעניינו של יום: הלכות פסח בפסח, הלכות עצרת בעצרת והלכות חג בחג.

Rishonim offer various answers to this contradiction. According to the **Ran,** the only obligation of studying the halachot related to the *chag* applies on the *chag* itself, while the Gemara in *Pesachim* is referring only to the fact that one who asks a halachic question about a holiday within thirty days is considered as asking a question on a timely topic (and answering him takes precedence).

☝ Ran, Megilla 2b (Pagination of the Rif)

Moshe enacted for the Jewish people that they should ask questions about and expound upon the subject of the day: The halachot of Pesach, etc. In other words, we ask questions about and explain their halachot. And that which we say elsewhere: One asks about the halachot of Passover thirty days before Passover, that is a different issue, as it does not mean that one is obligated to expound on the halachot of Pesach from that time. **Rather, it means to say that one who asks about them in the study hall during that time is called one who asks about a timely subject**…

3. ר"ן | מגילה ב: בדפי הרי"ף

"משה תיקן להם לישראל, שיהיו שואלין ודורשין בעניינו של יום: הלכות פסח וכו'". כלומר, ששואלין ומפרשין הלכותיהן. והא דאמרינן בעלמא: "שואלין בהלכות הפסח קודם לפסח ל' יום" – ההוא עניינא אחרינא הוא, דלאו למימר דמחייבין מהאי זימנא לדרוש בהלכות פסח אלא לומר שהשואל בהם **בבית המדרש באותו זמן מיקרי שואל כעניין**…

It seems from **Tosafot** though that they disagree with the Ran and hold that there is an obligation both to study the halachot for thirty days beforehand, as well as an obligation to study the halachot on the holiday itself.

☝ Tosafot, Megilla 4a, s.v. Mai

…Even Yom Tov, where we expound on it thirty days beforehand, even so, we expound on that day, as it is taught in a *baraita* (*Megilla* 32a), "Moshe related the holidays of Hashem," etc.

4. תוספות | מגילה ד. ד"ה מאי

…אפילו יום טוב דדרשינן שלשים יום לפניו ואפילו הכי דורשין בו ביום כדתניא (לקמן לב.) וידבר משה את מועדי ה' וכו'.

The **Beit Yosef** quotes the explanation of the Ran and then suggests the following additional explanation to resolve the contradiction.

🏠 Beit Yosef, Orach Chaim Siman 429

.5 בית יוסף | או"ח סימן תכט

ועוד יש לומר דדיני פסח על כל פנים צריך להודיעם לעם קודם לפסח שלשים יום כדי שיהיה להם שהות רב להתעסק בטחינת החיטים ואפיית מצה והגעלת כלים וביעור חמץ דאילו בפסח לית להו תקנתא אי לא עבדו להו כהלכתיהו מקמי הכי...

One can also answer that one must inform the people about the laws of Pesach thirty days before Pesach so that they will have a lot of time to engage in the grinding of the wheat and the baking of matzot and placing utensils in boiling water [hagala] and burning the chametz. As on Pesach, these have no rectification if they have not been properly performed according to the halacha beforehand…

והא דתניא ששואלין בהלכות פסח בפסח והלכות חג בחג היינו לדרוש בטעמים שבעבורם נצטוינו במועד ההוא וגם כן לדרוש בדברים שאסור ומותר לעשות ביום טוב.

And that which was taught that they should ask about the halachot of Pesach on Pesach, **that is referring to expounding on the reasons about which we were commanded [to observe] that holiday,** and also to expound on the activities that are forbidden and permitted to do on Yom Tov.

According to the *Beit Yosef*, the directive to study the halachot of Pesach thirty days prior to the *chag* refers to studying all of the halachot that relate to the preparation for the *chag*, while the statement concerning studying on the *chag* refers to the more philosophical reasons behind each holiday in general, as well as the laws of Yom Tov.[1]

The **Shulchan Aruch** simply quotes the language of the *baraita* in *Pesachim* almost word for word.

א Shulchan Aruch, Orach Chaim 429:1

.6 שולחן ערוך | או"ח תכט:א

שואלין בהלכות פסח קודם לפסח שלשים יום.

We inquire about the halachot of *Pesach* thirty days before Pesach.

The **Bi'ur Halacha** notes though that there are actually two versions of the text in the Gemara. One states "*sho'alin*," we inquire, while the other is "*sho'alin v'dorshin*," we inquire and expound. The latter is the version printed in our Gemara, while the second is the version found in some *Rishonim* as well as in the *Shulchan Aruch*. The *Bi'ur Halacha* then proceeds to explain how the difference between them stems from the different interpretations of this passage given in the *Rishonim* above.

---

1. According to this understanding, it would seem that this halacha may apply only to Pesach, but not to the other two festivals (Sukkot and Shavuot) where preparation is not needed beforehand (though perhaps Sukkot is different, since the *sukka* and *arba minim* do need to be prepared beforehand). The *Beit Yosef* here (s.v. *tanya*) also states explicitly that this is the case, though he offers a different reason for it that there are many more halachot of Pesach than there are of the other *chagim* (including Sukkot, concerning which he writes that it is not difficult to build a Sukka or purchase kosher *arba minim*). However, a number of *Acharonim* write that the custom is to study the halachot of the other festivals as well thirty days before (see *Bach, Magen Avraham,* and *Pri Chadash* to this *siman*). But there are different opinions about the issue (in addition to the discussion in the text of the nature of the halacha and whether one must actually study the halachot), and there is also further discussion concerning the other holidays (Purim, Chanukah, Rosh Hashana, etc.). See *Gra* (429:1), *Tosafot* (*Megilla* 4a s.v. *mai*), *Mishna Berura* (429:1) and *Piskei Teshuvot* (429:1). It is also interesting to note that the source in the Torah for this halacha focuses only on the halachot of the *korban Pesach* (since the subject is *Pesach Sheini*, concerning which no other halachot apply). Apparently, thirty days was necessary even concerning the *korban Pesach* alone. [Addition of the English editors]

א | Bi'ur Halacha, Orach Chaim 429:1

We inquire – In the *Tur* it states, "we inquire and expound," which is in accordance with the version of our Gemara in *Pesachim* 6a and *Bechorot* 58a. But in the Rif, the version is only "we inquire," and that is the version in *Avoda Zara* 5b and *Sanhedrin* 12b. **Now it would seem [at first glance] that there is no practical difference between them,** as both mean the same thing – to discuss the halachot of Pesach before Pesach. And that is what it says in Rashi in *Rosh Hashana* 7a and *Bava Kamma* 113a, that they would publicly expound on the laws of Pesach thirty days before Pesach.

But the Ran in the first chapter of *Pesachim* and the first chapter of *Megilla* says that when it says "we inquire," it means that **during this time, if two students came [to the teacher] and one asked about the halachot of Pesach, we address him first**… and his words are the [same as the] words of the Rashba at the end of the fourth chapter in *Megilla*.

But a number of *Rishonim* disagree with them: Rashi in a number of places, Tosafot in the first chapter of *Megilla* 4a, and the Rokeach – it is clear from all of them **that there is an obligation to expound on the halachot of Pesach thirty days before.** And so too in the *Ittur* it uses the version of "we inquire and expound," and likewise in the *Ohr Zarua*… and also the main idea of the Gemara proves this, since it does not make sense to say that people would degrade *chametz* simply because we address a student who asked a question first, since there is no publicity at all through answering a student who asks[2]… if so, we see that the opinion of the Ran and Rashba are a lone minority one against all of the *Rishonim* mentioned earlier… but nevertheless [even according to them], there is certainly an obligation to learn [the halachot of Pesach] thirty days before in groups in the *beit midrash*, even according to the words of the *Yerushalmi*[3]…

7. ביאור הלכה | או"ח תכט:א

שואלין וכו' – בטור איתא "שואלין ודורשין", והוא כגירסת הגמרא דילן בפסחים דף ו ובבכורות דף נח. וברי"ף הגירסא "שואלין" לבד, וכן הגירסא בעבודה זרה ובסנהדרין דף יב. **ולכאורה אין נפקא מינה בזה**, דכוונה אחת הוא – לישא וליתן בהלכות הפסח קודם הפסח. וכן איתא ברש"י ראש השנה דף ז ובבא קמא דף קיג, שהיו דורשין ברבים בהלכות הפסח קודם פסח ל' יום.

אכן בר"ן פרק קמא דפסחים ופרק קמא דמגילה אמר, דמה שאמר "שואלין" היינו, דבזה הזמן אם באו ב' תלמידים ואחד שאל בהלכות פסח – נזקקין לו קודם… ודבריו הן דברי הרשב"א בסוף פרק רביעי דמגילה.

אבל כמה וכמה ראשונים פליגי עלייהו: רש"י בכמה מקומות, ותוספות בפרק קמא דמגילה דף ד, והרוקח – בכולהו מבואר להדיא, **דחיוב לדרוש מקודם בהלכות פסח שלושים יום**. וכן ב"עיטור" העתיק הגירסא "שואלין ודורשין", וכן באור זרוע… וגם עיקר העניין מוכח כן, דאילו מפני שנזקקין לתלמיד ששואל כעניין – לא שייך לומר דמשום זה יזלזלו בחמץ, דאין כאן פרסום כלל בזה שמשיב לתלמיד כששואל… אם כן נמצא דעת הר"ן והרשב"א יחידאין הם נגד כל הראשונים הנזכרים לעיל… ועל כל פנים בבית המדרש בחבורות – בודאי יש חיוב ללמוד שלושים יום קודם, אף לדברי הירושלמי…

---

2. The *Bi'ur Halacha* is referring here to the Gemara in *Sanhedrin* 12b and elsewhere that mentions this notion of *sho'alin v'dorshin* thirty days before Pesach to prove that the Sanhedrin should not make a leap year on the last day of Adar (and make that Rosh Chodesh of Adar Sheni). Since they have already begun studying the halachot, they will not believe that it is a leap year and that Nissan is not starting yet, but will rather observe the coming month as Nissan, and violate the prohibition of *chametz* in the month afterward, which is the true month of Nissan. So the *Bi'ur Halacha* is saying that if the meaning of *sho'alin v'dorshin* is in accordance with the Ran, it is hard to understand why simply giving precedence to a student who asks about Pesach would cause people to refuse to believe that the next month was changed to Adar Sheni. Moreover, giving precedence to a student does not publicize the coming of Pesach sufficiently for the Gemara to utilize the concept in this context. [Addition of the English editors]

3. This is referring to a previous section of this passage in the *Bi'ur Halacha* (not brought in the quote here) that the *Yerushalmi* may limit the notion of studying the halachot of Pesach thirty days before to studying in groups at the *beit va'ad*, where everyone gathered together to study, similar to a *beit midrash*. So the *Bi'ur Halacha* states that the simple understanding of the *Bavli*

According to the *Bi'ur Halacha,* the majority opinion is that of Tosafot, and this is the halacha, that a real obligation indeed exists to study the halachot of Pesach beginning thirty days beforehand. Despite the strong argument of the *Bi'ur Halacha,* **Rav Ovadia Yosef** offers a lengthy defense of the Ran and rejects the opinion of the *Bi'ur Halacha* that the halacha does not follow the Ran. According to Rav Ovadia, there is no obligation to study and expound the halachot of Pesach thirty days before, though he adds that halachic authorities must be expert in these laws before the *chag* so that they can properly answer people's questions.

 ### Responsa Yabia Omer, Vol. 2, Orach Chaim 22:6

8. שו"ת יביע אומר | חלק ב, או"ח כב:ו

...And concerning the practical halacha: Our teacher the *Shulchan Aruch* rules that "we inquire about the halachot of *Pesach* thirty days before Pesach. And the *Mishna Berura* writes in the *Bi'ur Halacha* that from the fact that it says "we inquire [*sho'alin*]," and it does not say what it says in the *Tur* "we inquire and expound [*sho'alin v'dorshin*]," it seems that he holds like the answer of the Ran... and we find that the opinion of the Rashba and Ran are a lone minority opinion against all of the *Rishonim* mentioned earlier, this is the gist of his words.

But before I answer, I said to "perk up" the ear that in truth, many *poskim* hold like what the Rashba and Ran explained, and they are not the only ones with this [opinion] at all... we find before us a whole slew of "prophets who prophesize in one form," like one of the answers in the *Beit Yosef,* and as it says in the *Shulchan Aruch,* and they are: The Ramban, Rashba, Ritva, Ran, Maharam Chalava, Meiri, and Rashbetz... Therefore it seems in my humble opinion **that the accepted approach is like the opinion of the *Beit Yosef* and the *Shulchan Aruch,* that there is no absolute obligation to learn the halachot of Pesach from Purim and onward, and it is permitted for every Torah scholar to continue in his learning wherever his heart desires** (see *Avoda Zara* 19a; *Ma'amar Mordechai* 553). Nevertheless, those who issue halachic rulings to the public or who give *shiurim* spread Torah to the community of Hashem must learn these matters themselves and be expert in them to respond to those who ask about them, as "the word of Hashem," this refers to halacha.[4]

...ולעניין דינא: הנה פסק מרן בשולחן ערוך: "שואלין בהלכות פסח קודם לפסח שלושים יום". וכתב המשנה ברורה בביאור הלכה, דממה שנאמר "שואלין", ולא כתב כמו שכתוב בטור – "שואלין ודורשין" – משמע דסבירא ליה כתירוץ הר"ן (פרק קמא דפסחים)... ונמצא, שדעת הרשב"א והר"ן יחידאה הם נגד כל הראשונים הנזכרים לעיל. עד כאן תורף דבריו.

וטרם אענה אמרתי להעיר אוזן, כי באמת דעת הרבה פוסקים כמו שביארו הרשב"א והר"ן, ואינם יחידים בזה כלל.... נמצא לפנינו חבל נביאים המתנבאים בסגנון אחד, כתירוץ האחד של הבית יוסף, וכמו שכתוב גם כן בשולחן ערוך, הלא הם: הרמב"ן, והרשב"א, והריטב"א, והר"ן, ומהר"ם חלאווה, והמאירי והרשב"ץ...

(יב) לכן נראה לעניות דעתי, **שהעיקר כדעת מרן הבית יוסף והשולחן ערוך, שאין חיוב גמור ללמוד הלכות פסח מפורים ואילך, ומותר לכל תלמיד חכם להמשיך בלימודו במקום שליבו חפץ** (עיין עבודה זרה, דף יט עמוד א. ועיין במאמר מרדכי סימן תקנג סעיף קטן ב.) ומכל מקום המורים הוראות לרבים, או הנותנים שיעורים ומרביצי תורה לקהל.

---

does not appear to agree with this, but at the very least, we should accept the *Yerushalmi*'s understanding and not that of the Ran, according to whom no obligation to study the halachot exists at all. [Addition of the English editors]

4.   Rav Eliezer Melamed (*Peninei Halacha* pp. 13–14) concludes that since many opinions hold that one should study the halachot, it is certainly recommended to do so, though he agrees that the imperative is not absolute and not according to all opinions. [Addition of the English editors]

WHAT IS THE REASON FOR BEDIKAT CHAMETZ?

Let us now turn to the halachot of *bedikat chametz*, searching for *chametz* before Pesach. The **Mishna** at the beginning of **Masechet Pesachim** records the obligation to search for *chametz* on the night before Pesach.

Mishna, Pesachim 1:1	**9. משנה	פסחים א:א**

On the evening [*ohr*] of the fourteenth of the month of Nissan, **one searches for leavened bread** in his home **by candlelight. Any place into which one does not** typically **take leavened bread does not require a search,** as it is unlikely that there is any leavened bread there…

אור לארבעה עשר בודקים את החמץ לאור הנר. כל מקום שאין מכניסין בו חמץ – אין צריך בדיקה...

What is the specific reason why Chazal enacted this search for *chametz*? According to **Rashi**, the purpose is to ensure that one does not violate the prohibitions of owning *chametz* on Pesach, known as *bal yeira'eh ubal yimatzei*, which comes from the *pesukim* such as ולא יראה לך חמץ, "there should be no *chametz* seen for you," (*Shemot* 13:7), and שאור לא ימצא בבתיכם, "no leaven shall be found in your house" (*Shemot* 12:19).

Rashi, Pesachim 2a	**10. רש"י	פסחים ב.**

We search – So that one should not violate *bal yeira'eh* and *bal yimatzei*.

בודקין – שלא יעבור עליו ב"בל ייראה" וב"בל ימצא".

Tosafot though question Rashi on the premise that there cannot be a Torah violation here (and rabbinic *gezeirot* are usually instituted only when there is a concern of violating a *de'oraita*), since *mide'oraita*, on a Torah level, the *chametz* is rendered ownerless simply through *bitul chametz*, declaring the *chametz* to be nullified, as is clear from the **Gemara** later (*Pesachim* 6b). If so, why would Chazal feel the need to enact an additional institution of *bedikat chametz*? For this reason, Tosafot disagree with Rashi and hold that Chazal instituted this rule because they were concerned one may otherwise find pieces of *chametz* on Pesach and come to eat them (even if they were already nullified).

Tosafot, Pesachim 2a	**11. תוספות	פסחים ב.**

On the evening of the fourteenth, one searches for leavened bread – Rashi explains: So that he should not violate *bal yeira'eh* and *bal yimatzei*. But this is difficult for the Ri, since one requires nullification (*bitul*), as the Gemara states (6b):

אור לארבעה עשר בודקין את החמץ – פירש הקונטרס: "שלא לעבור עליו ב"בל ייראה' ו'בל ימצא'". וקשה לר"י, כיון דצריך ביטול, כדאמר בגמרא (ו:):

One who searches must nullify. And according to the Torah, *bitul* alone is sufficient; why then did they require *bedika* at all? And it seems to the Ri that even though *bitul* alone suffices, **the Sages were stringent to search for *chametz* and to destroy it so that one does not come to eat it.** And this is also evident from [the Gemara] later (10b) where Rava inquired: If there was a loaf of bread on a high beam, etc., or perhaps sometimes it falls and he will come to eat it[5]...

"הבודק צריך שיבטל", ומדאורייתא בביטול בעלמא סגי – אמאי הצריכו חכמים בדיקה כלל? ונראה לר"י, דאע"ג דסגי בביטול בעלמא החמירו חכמים לבדוק חמץ ולבערו שלא יבא לאכלו. וכן משמע לקמן (י:) דבעי רבא ככר בשמי קורה וכו' או דלמא זימנין דנפל ואתי למיכליה...

The **Ran** resolves the questions against Rashi and defends Rashi's explanation.

12. הר"ן על הרי"ף | פסחים א.

⬆ Ran on the Rif, Pesachim 1a

...One may answer **that on a biblical level, one of them is adequate,** meaning either *bedika* or *bitul*, as *bedika* alone is also effective... and any case where one searched, one need not nullify it according to the Torah. Therefore, it makes sense to say that the purpose of the *bedika* is so that one should not violate *bal yira'eh*, as the fact that the Sages required *bitul* following the *bedika* is only by rabbinic rule, perhaps one will find a nice piece of bread and his mind will be on it, as it says in the Gemara (6b),

...Rather, this is the essential idea: That which the Torah stated "you shall destroy [the *chametz*]" can be fulfilled in one of two ways. Either one can mentally nullify all of the *chametz* that one has in his possession, and remove it from his possession in his mind, and that is sufficient on a biblical level even for *chametz* that is known to him, or if he did not nullify it mentally at all, then he must biblically search for it in any place that it is normally found and destroy it.

Therefore, Rashi writes that we search for *chametz* in order not to violate *bal yira'eh* and *bal yimatzei*, but that is for one who does not nullify it. But one nullifies it, that is adequate. **But since this *bitul* is dependent upon people's thoughts, and they do not have the same thoughts [as each other], it is possible that they will be lenient and not remove it from their hearts entirely. [Therefore,] the Sages felt that one should be stringent that**

...ויש לומר, דמדאורייתא בחד מינייהו סגי, כלומר: או בבדיקה או בביטול, דבדיקה לחודה נמי מהניא... וכל שבדק מן התורה – אינו צריך לבטל. הלכך שפיר איכא למימר, דבדיקה אתי כדי שלא יעבור עליו בבל ייראה, שמה שהצריכו חכמים ביטול אחר הבדיקה אינו אלא מדבריהם, שמא ימצא גלוסקא יפהפיה ודעתיה עלויה, כדאיתא בגמרא (ו:),

...אלא כך הוא עיקרן של דברים: שזה שאמרה תורה "תשביתו", יכול להתקיים באחד משני דברים: או שיבטל בלבו כל חמץ שיש ברשותו, ויוציאנו במחשבתו מרשותו, וסגי בהכי מדאורייתא אפילו בחמץ הידוע לו, או אם לא בטלו בלבו כלל – צריך מן התורה שיבדוק אחריו בכל מקום שהוא רגיל להימצא שם, ויבערנו מן העולם.

ולפיכך כתב רש"י ז"ל שבודקין את החמץ, כדי שלא יעבור עליו בבל ייראה ובל יימצא, והיינו למי שאינו מבטל, אבל למי שמבטל – סגי בהכי, אלא מפני שביטול זה תלוי במחשבתן של בני אדם, ואין דעותיהן שוות, ואפשר שיקלו בכך ולא יוציאוהו מליבן לגמרי – ראו חכמים להחמיר שלא

---

5. Rava's question is whether one is required to take the effort to remove *chametz* located in a high place. On one hand, it probably will not fall, but on the other hand, if it does, perhaps the person might come to eat it. Since the Gemara assumes that if it falls, concern exists that the person might eat it, it appears that even where the *bitul* is recited, the concern applies. [Addition of the English editors]

bitul **is not adequate, and they required** *bedika* **and** *bi'ur* (destroying it)**, which is also sufficient on a biblical level, or** [they required *bedika* and *bi'ur*] **because they were concerned that if he left it in his house, he may come to eat it…** this is my opinion, and it is based on the approach of Rashi.

יספיק ביטול, והצריכוהו בדיקה וביעור, שהוא מספיק גם כן מן התורה, או מפני שחששו, שאם ישהנו בתוך ביתו יבוא לאכלו... זהו דעתי, והוא על דרך רש"י ז"ל.

According to the Ran, *bedika* is required on a rabbinic level (even though *bitul* is effective on a Torah level) either due to the concern that one may not sincerely nullify the *chametz,* but merely declare it ownerless while still mentally maintaining ownership, or the concern that one may mistakenly eat it on Pesach. **Rav Akiva Eiger** questions the first possible concern though for the following reason. There is a well-known halacha that *devarim sheb'leiv einan devarim,* mental thoughts are not considered halachically binding. If so, then one's verbal declaration to nullify the *chametz* should nevertheless be binding, even if one did not truly mean it.

Rav Akiva Eiger answers as follows:

א   Responsa Rabbi Akiva Eiger, Mahadura Kamma, Siman 23

13. שו"ת רבי עקיבא איגר | מהדורה קמא, סימן כג

…One must answer that the word *bitul* does not refer to actually becoming ownerless, rather it is just an indication of what is in one's heart, that one does not consider it significant, but rather one considers it like dust. So **since we are evaluating what is in one's heart, meaning in a manner of revealing his intent, then if that is not his intent, then the** *bitul is meaningless.* If so, we have a good reason why *hefker* is stronger than *bitul,* since [a declaration of] *hefker* will certainly cause the *chametz* to leave his possession, and if it were the opposite in his mind, it would be considered "matters of the heart."

...וצריך לומר, כיוון דבאמת לשון "ביטול" לא הווי הפקר ממש, רק גילוי דעת למה שבליבו, שאינו חושבו ונחשב לו כעפרא, וכיוון דאנו דנין על מה שבליבו, דהיינו בדרך גילוי מילתא מה שבדעתו, ואם בדעתו אינו כן – אין הביטול כלום. ואם כן יש לנו טעמא רבא דהפקר עדיף מביטול, דבהפקר בודאי יצא החמץ מרשותו, דלו יהא דהיה בלבו בהיפוך – הווי דברים שבלב.

RABBI AKIVA EIGER (1761–1837)

Rav Akiva Eiger was born in Eisenstadt (current day Austria). As a young boy, he was already recognized as being exceptionally bright, and at age 12, he was sent to study at the yeshiva of his uncle, Rav Wolf Eiger. At age 20, he married and settled in Lisa (his wife's hometown), where his father-in-law supported him and he established a small yeshiva. He was eventually appointed as the rabbi of Markisch-Friedland, located in what was then Prussia, a post he held for almost twenty-five years. During this time, his first wife Glickel passed away, for whom he mourned greatly. He wrote that they would often discuss matters of *yirat shamayim* together with her until very late at night. He later married his niece and together they gave birth to a number of additional children, one of whom became the second wife of the *Chatam Sofer.* Towards the end of his life, he was appointed as the rabbi of Posen, a big city with a very large and active Jewish community, and he remained in the position for twenty-two years until the day of his death.

Rav Akiva Eiger wrote a number of important works that are still studied carefully to this day. One of them is the *Gilyon HaShas,* brief notes containing sharp questions or comments on the Gemara, which is printed in all standard editions of the Vilna edition. Another is his comments on the *Shulchan Aruch,* which are also printed in standard editions of the *Shulchan Aruch,* and a third is his collection of responsa, which were sent to questioners all over Europe and remain relevant to many practical halachic issues today.

According to Rav Akiva Eiger, the *bitul* is not truly a verbal declaration. Instead, it simply discloses to all what the person's intentions are. Therefore, if one's intentions are not truly that the *chametz* become ownerless, then the *bitul* would not take effect. This is different than a true declaration of *hefker*, which would certainly take effect, even if the person did not mean it. For this reason, Rashi holds that *bedika* is required even if one recited the declaration of *bitul*.[6]

---

6. It should be noted that this is consistent with and explains the approach of Rashi (discussed later in the *shiur*) to *bitul* as a declaration that the *chametz* is worthless. But Tosafot hold (also discussed later) that *bitul* is in fact a declaration that the *chametz* is *hefker*. [Addition of the English editors]

THE TIME FOR BEDIKAT CHAMETZ AND THE ACCOMPANYING RESTRICTIONS

The Ideal Time for the *Bedika*

What is the reason that the obligation of *bedikat chametz* was instituted to be at night rather than in the daytime?[7] The **Gemara** in **Pesachim** gives two reasons for it.

Masechet Pesachim 4a	14.מסכת פסחים ד.

Rav Nachman bar Yitzchak said: One searches for leaven **in** the evening as it is **a time when people are found in their homes,** and they have the opportunity to perform the search. **And** furthermore, **the light of the lamp is favorable for** conducting a **search** specifically at night. As the search is conducted with a lamp, it is preferable to search at night.[8]

והשתא אמר רב נחמן בר יצחק: בשעה שבני אדם מצויין בבתיהם, ואור הנר יפה לבדיקה.

Which part of the night of the fourteenth is considered the ideal time for performing *bedikat chametz*? May it be done at any time of the night or must it be performed immediately after nightfall? According to the work known as the *Katuv Sham*, written by the **Ra'avad,** one should begin the *bedika* immediately after nightfall. He derives this from the fact that the Mishna uses the word *ohr* to describe this night, which means that one should perform the mitzva when there is still some light left in the sky, which would refer to the beginning of the evening.

Katuv Sham of the Ra'avad, Pesachim 1a (Pagination of the Rif)	15.כתוב שם לראב״ד | פסחים א. בדפי הרי״ף

… But the clear reason that all of the instances where one must [perform a mitzva] at the beginning of the night, such as *bedikat chametz* and lighting torches [to publicize

...אבל הטעם הברור שכל המקומות שהוא צריך להקדים לתחלת הלילה, כגון בדיקת החמץ ומשיאין משואות

---

7.   The issue of how to perform *bedikat chametz* in cases where one plans to be away for Pesach and leaves before the night of the fourteenth (the subject of the Gemara in the opening source of the *shiur*) is beyond the purview of this *shiur*. In brief, the basic accepted halacha is that if one leaves within thirty days of Pesach, one should perform the *bedika* on the night prior to departure using a candle and recite the *bitul* declaration afterwards that is usually recited on the night of the fourteenth. However, a *beracha* is not recited, and most do not require placing ten pieces of bread out either (*Shulchan Aruch* 436:1, *Mishna Berura* 436:3, *Piskei Teshuvot* 432:5). [Addition of the English editors]

8.   Although one could argue that the *bedika* should be done in the day, when the candlelight would be unnecessary, Rashi here notes that the Gemara (*Pesachim* 7b) derives from a number of *pesukim* that the search should take place with a candle specifically. This Gemara will be discussed further in the continuation of the *shiur*. Another point discussed by the *Rishonim* here is whether these two reasons are distinct and stand independently. According to some commentaries, the main reason is the first one, and therefore one could search during the day if one is home. But many commentaries hold that both reasons are important, and even if one were home, one should wait until nighttime to use a candle (see, e.g., *Chidushei Rabbeinu Dovid*). This is indeed the accepted halacha as well. [Addition of the English editors]

the new month] (*Rosh Hashana* 22b), it states *"ohr,"* is **because there is still some daylight left and it is not [totally] dark,** as it is written, "and He called the darkness nighttime" (*Bereishit* 1:5)…

(ראש השנה כב עמוד ב), תני "אור", מפני שעדיין יש שם אור היום ואינו חושך, כדכתיב "ולחושך קרא לילה" (בראשית א, ה)...

The **Shulchan Aruch,** as explained by the **Mishna Berura,** accepts this as the halacha that the *bedika* must take place at the beginning of the night.

א | Shulchan Aruch, Orach Chaim 431:1
16. שולחן ערוך | או"ח תלא:א

We search for *chametz* using a candle at the beginning of the evening of the fourteenth of Nissan, in the holes and crevices, in all places that it is normal to bring in *chametz*.

בתחלת ליל י"ד בניסן בודקים את החמץ לאור הנר, בחורין ובסדקין, בכל המקומות שדרך להכניס שם חמץ.

א | Mishna Berura, Orach Chaim 431:1
17. משנה ברורה | או"ח תלא:א

At the beginning of the evening, etc. – This means **immediately following nightfall, when there is still a small amount of daylight,** that is when it is proper to begin to search, so that one should not be lax about it or forget.[9]

בתחלת ליל וכו' – פירוש: תיכף אחר יציאת הכוכבים, שיש עדיין קצת מאור היום, ראוי להתחיל לבדוק, כדי שלא יתרשל או שלא ישכח.

Restrictions Prior to Performing the *Bedika*

The **Gemara** in **Pesachim** (in the continuation of the passage cited above) states that one should not begin studying Torah at nightfall for the same reason that the *Mishna Berura* in the previous source stated that one should begin the *bedika* shortly after nightfall – so the person should not forget to perform the *bedika*.

ח | Masechet Pesachim 4a
18. מסכת פסחים ד.

Abaye said: Therefore, a Torah scholar should not begin his regularly scheduled **period** of Torah study **in the evening** at the conclusion **of the thirteenth** of Nissan **that** is **the evening of the fourteenth,** as **perhaps he will become engrossed in the halacha** he is studying **and will come to be prevented from** performing the **mitzva** of searching for leaven.

אמר אביי: הילכך, האי צורבא מרבנן לא לפתח בעידניה באורתא דתליסר דנגהי ארבסר, דלמא משכא ליה שמעתיה ואתי לאימנועי ממצוה.

The problem with this ruling is that the **Gemara** in **Berachot** states that when a person returns home at night, they may study Torah prior to reciting the evening *Keriat Shema* and the *Ma'ariv* prayer if their regular practice is to study at that time.

---

9. See *Piskei Teshuvot* (431:7) who notes that there are some *nafka minot* whether the reason that the *bedika* should take place at the beginning of the evening is because this is the time instituted by Chazal ideally (the position of the Gra and *Taz* among others) or only because of concern that one may forget to do it (the position of the *Magen Avraham* among others, which is evident from the quote of the *Magen Avraham* below). These *nafka minot* include, e.g., whether one may appoint someone to remind him to do the *bedika* later. [Addition of the English editors]

ח Masechet Berachot 4b

19. מסכת ברכות ד:

...**But he will come from the field in the evening, enter the synagogue,** and until it is time to pray, he will immerse himself in Torah. **If he is accustomed to reading the Torah, he reads. If he is accustomed to learning** *mishnayot,* a more advanced level of study, **he learns. And** then **he recites** *Shema* **and prays...**

...אבל אדם בא מן השדה בערב, נכנס לבית הכנסת, אם רגיל לקרות קורא, ואם רגיל לשנות שונה, וקורא קריאת שמע ומתפלל...

Why is there no concern that one may forget to recite *Shema* in that case? There are at least two ways to resolve this question.

1. The ***Bach*** explains (O.C. 431:4) that since the mitzva of *Keriat Shema* occurs every day, one will not forget to recite it. But the mitzva of *bedikat chametz* occurs only once a year, so there is a chance that one may forget.
2. The ***Taz*** explains (431:2) that the proper time for *Keriat Shema* is all night, and ideally until midnight (in accordance with Rabban Gamliel in the first mishna in *Masechet Berachot*). Therefore, even if one's learning extends for a long time, one may still recite it afterward. But the mitzva of *bedikat chametz* begins immediately at the beginning of the night, as was previously explained, and that is the proper [time] for the mitzva.[10]

The ***Shulchan Aruch*** rules in accordance with the Gemara that studying Torah is forbidden before performing the *bedika* and adds that one should not eat or begin other significant activities either.

א Shulchan Aruch, Orach Chaim 431:2

20. שולחן ערוך | או"ח תלא:ב

Every person should be careful **not to begin any activity or eat before searching** [for *chametz*]. And even if one has a set time for study [of Torah], one should not study until one has searched [for *chametz*]...

יזהר כל אדם **שלא יתחיל בשום מלאכה ולא יאכל, עד שיבדוק.** ואפילו אם יש לו עת קבוע ללמוד, לא ילמוד עד שיבדוק...

The ***Mishna Berura*** comments that with regard to eating and other activities, the restriction takes effect already beginning a half an hour before nightfall, while with regard to Torah study, the *poskim* dispute whether it is permitted until nightfall.

א Mishna Berura, Orach Chaim 431:5, 7

21. משנה ברורה | או"ח תלא:ה, ז

Not to begin any activity, etc. – And it is even forbidden during the half hour prior to the time, lest one continue [past nightfall].

One should not study – With regard to this also, some forbid even during the half hour before, lest one continue for a long time, unless one requested from another to remind him when the time arrives. But some permit with regard to learning before [the time], and only when the time of nightfall arrives is it forbidden.

שלא יתחיל בשום מלאכה וכו' – ואפילו חצי שעה שקודם הזמן אסור דלמא אתי לאמשוכי.

לא ילמוד – גם בזה יש אוסרין אף בחצי שעה שמקודם דלמא אתי לאמשוכי הרבה אם לא שביקש לאחד שיזכירנו כשיבוא הזמן ויש מתירין לענין לימוד מקודם ורק בהגיע הזמן של צאת הכוכבים אסור.

10. The *Bach* cited here also suggests additional answers distinguishing between the two cases. [Addition of the English editors]

Must one stop studying Torah if one had already begun studying Torah before nightfall (or ½ hour before according to some)? According to the **Shulchan Aruch,** one need not stop when nightfall arrives in this case, while according to the **Rema,** one should stop, since the reason for the halacha is that one may be preoccupied with his learning and forget to perform the *bedika*. Consequently, there should be no distinction between the cases with respect to this concern.

א | Shulchan Aruch, Orach Chaim 431:2 | שולחן ערוך | או"ח תלא:ב .22

...And if he began to study while it was still day, he need not stop.

Rema: But some say that one must stop, and that seems to me to be the primary [opinion].[11]

...ואם התחיל ללמוד מבעוד יום, אין צריך להפסיק.

רמ"א: ויש אומרים שצריך להפסיק, וכן נראה לי עיקר.

Does the same halacha apply when one is learning in a *shiur* or study group in shul? Would all agree that one may not begin learning in a *shiur* after nightfall, or might they say that the halacha is different when learning in a group? The **Magen Avraham** suggests that in this case it is permitted to learn Torah, since there is no concern one studying in the shul will forget to return home – provided they are not engaged in analytical, in depth study.

א | Magen Avraham, Orach Chaim 431:5 | מגן אברהם | או"ח תלא:ה .23

...And those people who give a *dvar halacha* in the shul after *davening* **are permitted to deliver the shiur,** as it is specifically one who studies in his home that is forbidden, since he does not need to arise from his place. But this person [studying in shul] **will certainly go to his home** (Rabbi Avraham Chaim). But it seems to me that this is **specifically for one who recites a *dvar halacha* without analysis,** but it is forbidden to engage in *pilpul* analysis even if one is not in one's house, as in this case it certainly is logical to decree that perhaps his study will continue and he will refrain from [performing] the mitzva by forgetting to search afterwards.

...ואותן האנשים האומרים דבר הלכה בבית הכנסת אחר התפלה, **מותרין לומר השיעור,** דדוקא מי שלומד בביתו אסור שאינו מוכרח לקום ממקומו, אבל זה **בודאי ילך לביתו** (רבי אברהם חיים סימן ע"ט, כ"ה). ונראה לי, דדוקא **מי שאומר דבר הלכה בלא פלפול,** אבל אסור לעסוק בפלפול אפילו אינו בביתו, דבזה ודאי איכא למיגזר דילמא ממשכא ליה שמעתא ואתא לאימנועי ממצוה, שישכח אחר כך מלבדוק.

The **Yalkut Yosef** accepts this ruling as well and adds that the *gabbai* should remind everyone after the *shiur* to remember to search for *chametz*.

---

11. We should note that the *Acharonim* disagree over the interpretation of the opinion of the Rema. According to the flow of the *Shulchan Aruch* and the Rema based on how we have explained it, it would seem that the Rema holds that one must stop even if one began during the day, since Chazal instituted that the *bedika* be performed specifically at the beginning of the evening. Therefore, one is not permitted to continue if by doing so one will thereby violate the enactment of Chazal. This is the approach of the *Shulchan Aruch HaRav* (431:6, *Kuntres Acharon*) and the Gra (431:8), and is alluded to by the *Mishna Berura* (431:10). But the *Magen Avraham* (431:8) argues that the Rema only requires one to stop learning if one began during the half-hour prior to nightfall. But if one began earlier than that, one may continue.

Yalkut Yosef, Orach Chaim 431:7

Nevertheless, it is proper that at the conclusion of the *shiur*, the *gabbai* should announce and remind the participants in the *shiur* that they should go search for *chametz*. But even in public, they only permitted halachic rulings, or *daf yomi*, or *mishnayot*, without any *pilpul*, as is customary for *ba'alei batim* (working individuals), but not *pilpul*, lest they become carried away with the *pilpul* and forget to search.

ז:תלא ח"או | יוסף ילקוט .24

ומכל מקום טוב שעם סיום השיעור, יכריז ויזכיר השמש שהמשתתפים בשיעור ילכו לבדוק החמץ. אלא שגם ברבים לא התירו אלא פסקי הלכות, או דף יומי, או שיעור משניות, בלי פלפול, כנהוג בזה לבעלי בתים, אבל פלפול לא, שמא ימשכו אחרי הפלפול, וישכחו לבדוק.

> What type of eating is forbidden before the *bedika*? According to the **Yalkut Yosef,** only eating food that could constitute an actual meal is included is included in the restriction. Therefore, one may not eat the size of a *k'beitza* (an egg) of bread or grains.

Yalkut Yosef, Orach Chaim 431:3

It is forbidden to eat a meal of bread of more than the size of an egg [without its shell] prior to *bedikat chametz*, beginning from a half hour before the time for the *bedika*. And the status of cake is equivalent to that of bread. But it is permitted to eat up to a *k'beitza* of bread [without its shell, which is approximately 50 grams]. And it is permitted to eat fruits and vegetables even more than the size of a *k'beitza*, as well as a dish of rice and the like, and tea and coffee are permitted.

ג:תלא ח"או | יוסף ילקוט .25

אסור לאכול סעודה של פת יותר משיעור כביצה [בלי קליפתה], קודם בדיקת החמץ, החל מחצי שעה קודם זמן הבדיקה. ודין העוגה כדין הפת. אבל לאכול פת עד שיעור כביצה [בלי קליפתה, כחמשים גרם] מותר. ופירות וירקות מותר אפילו יותר מכביצה, וכן תבשיל אורז וכיוצא, אותה וקפה, מותר.

> The **Mishna Berura** agrees with this ruling as well but adds that after nightfall, one should not eat a lot of fruits or vegetables either.

א Mishna Berura, Orach Chaim 431:6

Should not eat – But mere tasting [i.e., not a meal] is permitted, and that means a *k'beitza* of bread but no more, or even lots of fruits, as we wrote at the end of *siman* 232... and see the *Bi'ur Halacha* that a significant amount of fruits are only permitted in the half-hour before the *bedika*, but when the time for *bedika* arrives, it is not proper to wait a lot while eating fruits.

ו:תלא ח"או | ברורה משנה .26

ולא יאכל – וטעימה בעלמא שרי והיינו פת כביצה ולא יותר או פירות אפילו הרבה וכמו שכתבנו בסוף סימן רלב עיין שם במשנה ברורה ועיין בבאור הלכה דפירות הרבה אינו מותר רק בהחצי שעה שקודם הבדיקה אבל משהגיע זמן הבדיקה גם על ידי פירות אין נכון לשהות הרבה.

> Another question that sometimes arises is what to do if one cannot be home at the time for *bedikat chametz*. For example, what should one do if one is still at work at that time? **Rav Ben Zion Abba Shaul** in his **Ohr L'tzion** discusses the proper practice in such a case.

Responsa Ohr L'tzion 3:7:2

27. שו"ת אור לציון | ג:ז:ב

Answer: One who wishes to remain in the store may appoint his wife or household members to search for the *chametz* at the proper time, and he should search the store if it requires searching. But if he cannot find someone to search for *chametz* at the right time, he must close the store at nightfall and return home for *bedikat chametz.*

תשובה: הרוצה להשאר בחנות, יכול למנות את אשתו או בני ביתו לבדוק את החמץ בזמן. ויבדוק הוא את החנות אם היא חייבת בבדיקה. אבל אם אינו מוצא מי שיבדוק לו את החמץ בזמנו, צריך לסגור את החנות בצאת הכוכבים, וללכת לביתו לבדיקת חמץ.

According to the *Ohr L'tzion,* one may appoint another to perform the *bedika* at home, but if that is impossible, one must leave work early in order to perform the mitzva.

WHERE MUST BEDIKAT CHAMETZ BE PERFORMED?

According to the **Gemara** in *Pesachim*, the obligation of *bedikat chametz* applies to any place in the house into which *chametz* may have been brought, while places into which *chametz* is not usually brought need not be searched.

Masechet Pesachim 8a

The Mishna stated that **any place into which one does not** typically **take** leaven does not require searching. The Gemara asks: **What** does the inclusive phrase: **Any place,** come **to include?** The Gemara answers that it comes **to include that which the Sages taught** in a *baraita*: **The upper and lower holes** in the wall of a house that are difficult to use, as well as **a veranda roof, a closet roof, a cowshed,** chicken **coops, a storehouse for straw, a wine cellar, and a storeroom for oil;** all these **do not require** that a **search** be conducted...

Rabba bar Rav Huna said: A salt storage and a storage for candles require searching for leaven, as one might have entered those storages during a meal. **Rav Pappa** likewise **said: A wood storage and a storage for dates require searching** for the same reason.

28. מסכת פסחים ח.

"כל מקום שאין מכניסין בו חמץ – אין צריך בדיקה". "כל מקום" לאתויי מאי? – לאתויי הא דתנו רבנן: חורי בית העליונים והתחתונים, וגג היציע, וגג המגדל, ורפת בקר, ולולין, ומתבן, ואוצרות יין, ואוצרות שמן – אין צריכין בדיקה...
אמר רבה בר רב הונא: בי מילחי ובי קירי צריך בדיקה. אמר רב פפא: בי ציבי ובי תמרי צריך בדיקה.

The **Shulchan Aruch** codifies this as the accepted halacha as well.

Shulchan Aruch, Orach Chaim 433:3

One searches all of the locations that one suspects *chametz* **may have been brought into them.** Therefore, all rooms in the house and the attics require *bedika*, since a person sometimes enters them with bread in his hand. But wine cellars from which a person does not [usually] take, and a storehouse for straw and the like, do not require *bedika*.

29. שולחן ערוך | או"ח תלג:ג

בודק כל המקומות שיש לחוש שמא הכניסו בהם חמץ. ולכן כל חדרי הבית והעליות צריכים בדיקה; שפעמים אדם נכנס בהם ופתו בידו. אבל אוצרות יין שאין מסתפק מהם, וכן מתבן וכיוצא בו, אינם צריכים בדיקה.

There are a number of other areas of one's house and property about which questions concerning *bedikat chametz* apply. One of them involves one's books and *sefarim*. Must one open and search through them on the chance that it may contain crumbs of *chametz*? According to the **Chazon Ish** and **Rav Mordechai Eliyahu,** one is indeed obligated to search through one's bookshelves of *sefarim* and books the same way one must search other parts of one's house.

Chazon Ish, Orach Chaim 116:18

 .30 חזון איש | או"ח קטז:יח

...It seems that concerning the obligation of a separation that the Sages instituted, as stated earlier,[12] there is no distinction between crumbs and a nice loaf of bread. **Therefore, one is obligated to search the *sefarim* due to the possibility of crumbs, even if they do not contain a *kezayit*.**

...נראה דלענין חיוב מחיצה שתיקנו חכמים, כדאמר לעיל, אין חילוק בין פירורין לגלוסקא יפה, והלכך חייבין לבדוק את הספרים משום חשש פירורין, אף שאין בהם כזית.

But others such as **Rav Ovadia Yosef** and **Rav Ben Zion Abba Shaul** hold that there is no obligation to search all of one's *sefarim*, and doing so is considered an additional (unrequired) stringency. Rather, one may simply nullify the *chametz* inside of them.

 Responsa Yabia Omer, Vol. 7, Orach Chaim 43

.31 שו"ת יביע אומר | חלק ז, או"ח מג

...But according to what was explained earlier from the *Rishonim* and *Acharonim*, **it is a very great stringency, and there is no basis for it in halacha, and no one is concerned with it at all,** and we do not see any senior rabbis who are devout with their Creator who are concerned with this at all. And go see what the people do. And I saw that my friend... HaGaon Rav Ben Zion Abba Shaul in Responsa *Ohr L'tzion* briefly noted this point in relation to the *Chazon Ish*... **that the bread crumbs inside *sefarim* are *batel* (nullified) in their small size, and with [the recital of] the *bitul* of "kol chamira" it is certainly adequate.** And one need not place a separation in front of the *sefarim* that one used during the meal during the rest of the year. **And it is permitted to learn with them on Pesach without searching for crumbs of *chametz* that may have fallen inside.** And this is the correct practical halacha.[13]

...אולם לפי המבואר לעיל מהראשונים והאחרונים חומרא יתרה היא מאד, ואין לזה שום יסוד בהלכה, ולית דחש להא כלל. ולא חזינן לרבנן קשישאי המתחסדים עם קונם שיחושו לכך כלל וכלל. ופוק חזי מאי עמא דבר. וכן ראיתי לידידי... הגרב"צ אבא שאול (נר"ו) [זצ"ל] בשו"ת אור לציון (חלק א סימן לב), שהעיר כן בקצרה על דברי החזון איש הנ"ל... שפירורי פת שבספרים בטלי במיעוטייהו, ובביטול כל חמירא בודאי דסגי להו. ואין צורך להעמיד מחיצה בפני הספרים שנשתמשו בהם בכל ימות השנה בשעת סעודה. ומותר ללמוד בהם בפסח מבלי לבדוק אחר פירורי חמץ שנפלו לתוכם. וכן עיקר להלכה ולמעשה.

Rav Shimon Eider in his English work on the halachot of Pesach mentions the opinion of the *Chazon Ish* as well as an in-between opinion of **Rav Moshe Feinstein** that although one need not search the *sefarim*, one should not bring those *sefarim* used around *chametz* to the table on Pesach. Rav Eider also adds that *bentchers* and the like that are often used near *chametz* should be sold, since they are often very difficult to clean.

---

12. This is a reference to the Gemara (*Pesachim* 6a) that states that one who has *chametz* in one's house that belongs to a gentile must erect a separation that is ten *tefachim* high next to it. The point of the *Chazon Ish* is that in his view, the separation must be erected even for crumbs of *chametz* (even though the Gemara also states that crumbs of *chametz* are not significant). Therefore, one must also search for crumbs in places where they are likely to be found, such as within the *sefarim*. [Addition of the English editors]

13. Rav Shlomo Zalman Auerbach (*Halichot Shlomo*, Pesach ch. 5, *dvar halacha* 10, also cited in the Dirshu edition of the *Mishna Berura* 433:14, 20) also holds that one need not check the *sefarim*, based on a comment of the *Sha'ar HaTziun* (433:33) who seems to indicate that one need not search for crumbs that are less than the size of a *kezayit*.

32. Rav Shimon Eider, Halachos of Pesach p. 72

Some *poskim* hold that *seforim* and books require *bedikah* [or a partition]. Other *poskim* hold that although *bedikah* is not required, one should not bring to the table on Pesach a volume which may have been used around *chometz*.[14] *Bentchilach* and *zemiros* booklets cannot be cleaned properly from *chometz* and should not be used during Pesach. They should be put away with the *chometz* which is sold to the gentile.[15]

The **Yalkut Yosef** notes (as do other *poskim*) that one must search one's car as well during the *bedikat chametz*.

 Yalkut Yosef, Orach Chaim 433:6

33. ילקוט יוסף | או"ח תלג:ו

One who has a private car must search it on the night of the four-teenth by candlelight, as per the mitzva of Chazal, even though the car is cleaned well before the night of the fourteenth. And even if one does not wish to use the car on any of the days of Pesach, one must search for *chametz*. Similarly, public buses and airplanes belonging to Israeli-owned airlines must search for *chametz* on the night of the fourteenth of Nissan, even if it had been cleaned well beforehand. Nevertheless, when one searches one's car, one need not recite the *beracha* of *al bi'ur chametz* again. Rather, the *beracha* he recited in his home at the time of the *bedika* suffices.

מי שיש לו מכונית פרטית, צריך לבדקה בליל י"ד לאור הנר, כמצות חז"ל. ואף על פי שמנקים היטב את המכונית לפני ליל י"ד. ואפילו אינו רוצה להשתמש במכונית בכל ימי הפסח, צריך לבדוק אותה מן החמץ. וכן בעלי אוטובוסים ציבוריים ומטוסים של חברות תעופה ישראליות חייבים לבדוק החמץ בליל י"ד ניסן אף שניקו אותם היטב קודם לכן. ומכל מקום כשבא לבדוק במכונית אין לו לחזור ולברך "על ביעור חמץ", אלא די במה שבירך בביתו בשעת הבדיקה.

In addition to searching one's house, the **Shulchan Aruch** rules that one must also search the shul, which is cautioned even more strongly by the **Mishna Berura**.

א **Shulchan Aruch, Orach Chaim 433:10**

34. שולחן ערוך | או"ח תלג:י

The shuls and study halls require a *bedika* since the children bring *chametz* into them.

בתי כנסיות ובתי מדרשות צריכים בדיקה, מפני שהתינוקות מכניסים בהם חמץ.

---

14. Rav Eider (footnote 68) cites this in the name of an oral ruling from Rav Moshe Feinstein, and also references *Igrot Moshe* (o.c. 1:145). [Addition of the English editors]

15. This *machloket* of whether one must search for crumbs in *sefarim* may be related to a much wider *machloket* concerning whether the obligation of *bedika* and *bi'ur chametz* applies to crumbs that are less than the size of a *kezayit*. Some *Acharonim* hold that even concerning these halachot, crumbs are considered insignificant, as the Gemara (6b) states. This appears to be the opinion of the *Sha'ar HaTziun* cited above and Rav Shlomo Zalman Auerbach. But the *Chayei Adam* (119:6) holds that one must search for and destroy even small crumbs, as the concern that one may come to eat them is still in effect. See also the *Mishna Berura* (442:33), which appears to present both sides of this question, and it is discussed by contemporary *poskim* as well (see the *Dirshu Mishna Berura* cited in footnote 12 above; *Piskei Teshuvot* 431:4). This dispute may have major implications for Pesach cleaning in general, as according to the more lenient opinion, one would not need to clean in a manner that ensures all small crumbs are disposed of, just edible crumbs that are the size of a *kezayit*, while the stringent opinion would disagree. It is also worthwhile to note that the *Piskei Teshuvot* there cites *Siddur Pesach K'hilchato* that even according to the stringent opinion, very small crumbs found in between the tiles on the floor (and in any similar place) are not included in the obligation for *bedika*, as no one would ever come to eat them due to their size plus the fact that they have likely been there for a long time and are completely inedible. On the other hand, places where one might find small foods that are still potentially edible like Cheerios (or similar type of food) may be a good example of cases subject to the dispute above (since some children might eat them if found on the floor). [Addition of the English editors]

35. משנה ברורה | או"ח תלג:מג

א Mishna Berura, Orach Chaim 433:43

Require *bedika* – On the night of the fourteenth by candle-light. But the attendants are not careful to search at night, but just sweep well during the day, but they are not acting properly, and one must warn them that they should fulfill the mitzva of the Sages properly, and they may recite a *beracha* on this *bedika*,[16] though they do not need to nullify [the *chametz*] after the *bedika*, since they cannot nullify and render ownerless *chametz* that is not theirs. And if one transgressed and did not search the shuls and study halls on the night of the fourteenth, one may search them *lechatchila* on the day of the fourteenth in daylight, and it is not necessary to search by candlelight, since they often have many windows, and there is a lot of light, and their status is like a portico explained in *se'if* 1[17]…

צריכים בדיקה – בליל י"ד לאור הנר. והשמשים אינם נזהרים לבדוק בלילה אלא מכבדין היטב ביום ולא יפה הם עושים וצריך להזהירם על כרחם שיקיימו מצות חכמים כתיקונה, ויכולים לברך על בדיקה זו אבל אינם צריכים לבטל אחר הבדיקה, לפי שאינם יכולים לבטל ולהפקיר חמץ שאינו שלהם. ואם עבר ולא בדק בתי כנסיות ובתי מדרשות בליל י"ד – יכול לבודקם לכתחלה ביום י"ד לאור היום, ואין צריך לבדוק לאור הנר, לפי שדרך להרבות בהם חלונות ויש בהם אורה גדולה ודינם כדין אכסדרה שנתבאר בסעיף א' [אחרונים]...

Another question that often arises is whether one must still perform *bedikat chametz* if one has spent much time thoroughly cleaning the entire house in the days and weeks leading up to Pesach. According to the **Shulchan Aruch,** it seems that even in this case, *bedikat chametz* must still be performed on the night of the fourteenth.

36. שולחן ערוך | או"ח תלג:יא

א Shulchan Aruch, Orach Chaim 433:11

One who sweeps his room on the thirteenth of Nissan and [while doing so] intends to search for *chametz* and to destroy it and is careful not to bring in more *chametz* [afterward] **must nevertheless search on the night of the fourteenth.**

Rema: Everyone must sweep his rooms prior to the *bedika*. And the pockets of one's clothing in which one occasionally puts *chametz* require *bedika*.

המכבד חדרו בי"ג בניסן ומכוין לבדוק החמץ ולבערו ונזהר שלא להכניס שם עוד חמץ – **אף על פי כן צריך לבדוק בליל י"ד.** הגה: וכל אדם צריך לכבד חדריו קודם הבדיקה. והכיסים או בתי יד של בגדים שנותנים בהם לפעמים חמץ, צריכין בדיקה.

Despite the fact that one must still perform a *bedika* nowadays, many poskim, including **Rav Shlomo Zalman Auerbach,** suggest that the manner in which the *bedika* is done after cleaning the house thoroughly may indeed be different than how it was originally performed.

---

16. Many *poskim* disagree with this ruling and hold that it is preferable not to recite a separate *beracha* on a *bedika* performed in the shul (*Aruch HaShulchan* 433:12; *Chovat HaDar*; *Maharsham* 5:49, cited in the *Piskei Teshuvot* 433:6). Rav Shimon Eider (*Halachos of Pesach* p. 73) also writes that such a practice is questionable. Therefore, the more accepted recommendation is for the one searching there to have in mind when reciting the *beracha* at home that it includes the *bedika* to be done in the shul as well (*Piskei Teshuvot* 433:6, citing the *Da'at Torah*). [Addition of the English editors]

17. The *Sha'ar HaTziun* (433:54) clarifies though that in corners where the sunlight does not reach one must still use a candle. The same should apply to a shul that does not have large windows or places in the shul that are not close to the windows. [Addition of the English editors]

Dirshu Edition of the Mishna Berura, Orach Chaim 433, Note 38

But in our times, where we sweep, wash, and clean extremely well, Rav Shlomo Zalman writes (*Halichot Shlomo*, Pesach 5:1) that there is no obligation to carefully inspect every single place [in the house] during the *bedika*, since that has already been done when they cleaned during the days prior to Pesach. The obligation of *bedika* in our times is to check carefully and evaluate whether they indeed cleaned well. This is also the opinion of Rav Yosef Shalom Eliashiv (*Halichot V'hanhagot al Hilchot Pesach*).[18]

37. משנה ברורה בהוצאת "דרשו" | או"ח תלג, הערה לח

אכן בזמננו שמכבדים ושוטפים ומנקים היטב היטב, כתב הגאון רב שלמה זלמן (הליכות שלמה פסח ה:א) שאין חובה לפשפש בשעת הבדיקה בכל המקומות, שכבר עשו כן בזמן שניקו בימים שקודם הפסח, וחובת הבדיקה בזמנינו היא לדקדק ולבחון בכל המקומות אם כן ניקו אותם היטב, וכן דעת הגאון רב יוסף שלום אלישיב (הליכות והנהגות על הלכות פסח).

---

18. The *Sha'arei Teshuva* here also mentions a similar custom of searching quickly during the *bedika* without carefully inspecting every nook and cranny. This source is mentioned by the *Piskei Teshuvot* (citing the *Da'at Torah* and Responsa *Kinyan Torah*) as an additional support for the custom nowadays of searching more quickly throughout the house, as otherwise it would take an inordinate amount of time to carefully search the entire house again (especially given that our houses today are generally much larger than houses in earlier times). [Addition of the English editors]

THE PROCEDURE FOR BEDIKAT CHAMETZ

Reciting the *Beracha*

Before beginning the actual *bedika*, one recites a *beracha* on the mitzva, just like other mitzvot. The **Gemara** in **Pesachim** quotes a dispute as to the proper text of the *beracha*.

Masechet Pesachim 7a | 38. מסכת פסחים ז.

Rav Yehuda said: One who searches for leaven **must recite a blessing.** The Gemara asks: **What blessing does he recite,** i.e., what is the correct formula of the blessing? **Rav Pappi said in the name of Rava** that one **recites:** Who has made us holy through His mitzvot and has commanded us **to remove leavened bread [*l'va'er chametz*]. Rav Pappa said in the name of Rava:** One should recite: **Concerning the removal of leavened bread [*al bi'ur chametz*].**

The Gemara comments: **With regard to** the formula: **To remove, everyone agrees that** it **certainly refers to the future.** This formulation undoubtedly indicates that the person reciting the blessing is about to begin fulfilling the mitzva of removing leaven, and it is therefore an appropriate blessing. **Where they disagree is with regard to** the formula: **Concerning the removal** of leaven. One **Sage,** Rav Pappi, **maintains** that **it is referring to** an act that was performed **previously.** Since this formula is referring to the removal of leaven as a task already completed, it would be more appropriate for a blessing recited after performance of that mitzva was completed. **And** the other **Sage,** Rav Pappa, **maintains** that this expression **refers to the future.** The Gemara concludes: **And the *halacha* is** that one should recite: **Concerning the removal of leaven,** as that expression is referring to the future as well.

אמר רב יהודה הבודק צריך שיברך. מאי מברך? רב פפי אמר משמיה דרבא (אומר) לבער חמץ רב פפא אמר משמיה דרבא על ביעור חמץ.

בלבער כולי עלמא לא פליגי דודאי להבא משמע, כי פליגי בעל ביעור מר סבר מעיקרא משמע ומר סבר להבא משמע. והלכתא על ביעור חמץ.

The accepted halacha is that the text of the *beracha* is *"al bi'ur chametz,"* as recorded by the **Shulchan Aruch** based on the conclusion of the Gemara. The *Shulchan Aruch* adds that one should not speak about matters unrelated to the *bedika* from the time that the *beracha* is recited until one completes the *bedika*.

Shulchan Aruch, Orach Chaim 432:1 | 39. שולחן ערוך | או"ח תלב:א

Shulchan Aruch: Before one begins to search, one recites the *beracha* of "who has sanctified us with his mitzvot and commanded us on burning the *chametz.*"

Rema: And if he began without a *beracha,* he should recite the *beracha* as long as he has not completed his search.

Shulchan Aruch: And one should be careful not to speak between the *beracha* and the beginning of the search. And it is best not to speak about other matters until he has completed the entire *bedika* so that he will keep in mind to search in every place that *chametz* is brought in.

שו"ע: קודם שיתחיל לבדוק יברך אשר קדשנו במצותיו וצונו על ביעור חמץ.

רמ"א: ואם התחיל לבדוק בלא ברכה יברך כל זמן שלא סיים בדיקתו.

שו"ע: ויזהר שלא ידבר בין הברכה לתחילת הבדיקה, וטוב שלא ידבר בדברים אחרים עד שיגמור כל הבדיקה כדי שישים אל לבו לבדוק בכל המקומות שמכניסין בו חמץ.

> Why is the *beracha* recited on the act of *bi'ur*, burning the *chametz*, rather than the *bedika* itself? The ***Mishna Berura*** explains the answer.

Mishna Berura, Orach Chaim 432:3 | 40. משנה ברורה | או"ח תלב:ג

On burning the *chametz* – Because even though he does not burn it until the next day, nevertheless since this search is for the purpose of burning it, it is considered similar to the *bi'ur* [and one may recite the *beracha* on the *bi'ur*]. And one cannot recite the *beracha* "*al bedikat chametz*" since this is not the conclusion of the mitzva, and one also cannot recite "*al bitul chametz*" since the primary nullification is dependent upon one's heart, and one does not recite a *beracha* on matters of the heart.

על ביעור חמץ – דאף על גב דאינו מבער עד למחר מכל מקום כיון דבדיקה זו לצורך ביעור הוי מעין הביעור ואין מברכין על בדיקת חמץ דאין זה סוף מצותו וגם אין מברכין על ביטול חמץ כיון דעיקר הביטול תלוי בלב ואין מברכין על דברים שבלב.

Using a Flashlight

We mentioned above that one should use a candle during the *bedika* to ensure that one can find any *chametz* that may remain in cracks and crevices that are otherwise hard to see. Is it permitted to use a flashlight either together with or instead of a candle? On one hand, the **Gemara** cites a number of *pesukim* as allusions to searching with a candle (some of which are quoted below). On the other hand, the reasons given by the Gemara there as to why a candle is more effective than searching with a large torch or sunlight, including the fact that it illuminates corners and crevices well and is not as dangerous, are certainly applicable to a flashlight as well.

⓷ Masechet Pesachim 7b–8a

41. מסכת פסחים ז:–ח.

The school of Rabbi Yishmael taught: On the night of the fourteenth one searches for leavened bread by the light of the lamp. Although there is no absolute proof for this matter, there is an allusion to this matter, as it is stated: "Seven days leaven shall not be found in your houses," and it says: "And he searched, starting with the eldest, and ending with the youngest; and the goblet was found." And it says: "At that time I will search Jerusalem with lamps," and it says: "The spirit of man is the lamp of God, searching all the inward parts."

The Sages taught: One does not search for leaven, neither by the light of the sun, nor by the light of the moon, nor by the light of a torch. Rather, the search should be conducted by the light of a lamp. The Gemara asks: And is the light of a torch not bright enough for searching?… And likewise Rava said: One who uses a torch for the blessing over fire in *havdala* has performed the mitzva in the optimal manner. Apparently, the light of a torch is greater than that of a lamp.

Rav Nachman bar Yitzchak said: The *baraita* does not prohibit the use of a torch due to its failure to provide

תנא דבי רבי ישמעאל לילי ארבעה עשר בודקים את החמץ לאור הנר אף על פי שאין ראיה לדבר זכר לדבר שנאמר שבעת ימים שאר לא ימצא ואומר ויחפש בגדול החל ובקטן כלה ואומר בעת ההיא אחפש את ירושלים בנרות ואומר נר (אלהים) [ה'] נשמת אדם חפש.

תנו רבנן אין בודקין לא לאור החמה ולא לאור הלבנה ולא לאור האבוקה אלא לאור הנר מפני שאור הנר יפה לבדיקה... ואבוקה לא והאמר רבא... ואמר רבא אבוקה להבדלה מצוה מן המובחר

אמר רב נחמן בר יצחק זה יכול להכניסו לחורין ולסדקין וזה אינו יכול להכניסו לחורין ולסדקין. רב זביד אמר זה אורו לפניו וזה אורו לאחריו. רב פפא אמר האי בעית והאי לא בעית רבינא אמר האי משך נהורא והאי מיקטף איקטופי.

sufficient light. Rather, it is due to the fact that one can put this lamp into holes and crevices, as it is a small flame, and one cannot put that torch into holes and crevices, as it is a large flame. Rav Zevid said: This lamp projects its light before it, facilitating the search, and that torch projects its light behind it, on the person conducting the search. Rav Pappa said: The reason is that when using this torch one fears starting a fire, and when using that lamp he does not fear starting a fire. Ravina said: This lamp consistently draws light, and the light of that torch fluctuates. Although overall the torch provides greater light than a lamp, it is less effective for use in a search.

Rav Eliezer Melamed holds that one may use a flashlight for the *bedika* since all of the reasons why the Gemara says that a candle must be used apply to a flashlight as well, though he notes that some are more *machmir* (stringent) since the Gemara derives using a candle from *pesukim*. He concludes that in places where it may be dangerous to use a candle, it is actually preferable to use a flashlight.

⓸ Peninei Halacha, Pesach pp. 43–44

42. פניני הלכה, פסח עמ' 43–44

It is permitted according to the strict halacha to search using a flashlight, since the reason for the enactment [to use a candle] is that its light is concentrated, and the light of a flashlight is also concentrated. And there is even an advantage to a flashlight that there is less concern that it may

לאור פנס, מצד הדין מותר לבדוק, מפני שטעם התקנה לבדוק לאור הנר מפני שאורו ממוקד, וכן אור הפנס ממוקד. ואף יש מעלה בפנס, שאין חשש שישרוף או ילכלך,

And if it is a good flashlight, its light is strong and concentrated even more than a candle. But some are stringent not to search with a flashlight, since the Sages derived from *pesukim* that the search should be performed with a candle. However, a flashlight could also be considered a candle, since the thread of the filament is the flame, and the battery is the oil (*She'arim Hametzuyanim B'halacha* 111:4).

In practice, the widespread custom is to search using a candle as Chazal were accustomed to doing, but the halacha is that anyone who wishes to search with a flashlight is allowed to do so, and in places where there the one searching is specifically concerned that the flame of the candle will cause a fire, it is preferable to use a flashlight (*Pesachim* 7b; see *She'arim Hametzuyanim B'halacha* 111:4; *Sefer Siddur Pesach K'hilchato* 13:10; *Yechaveh Da'at* 1:4).[19]

ואם הוא פנס טוב, אורו חזק וממוקד יותר מנר.
ויש מהדרים שלא לבדוק לאור פנס, משום שלמדו חכמים מן הפסוקים שחיפוש ראוי שיעשה לאור נר. אלא שגם פנס יכול להחשב כנר, שחוט הלהט הוא הלהבה, והסוללה – שמן.

למעשה, המנהג הרווח לבדוק לאור נר כפי שנהגו חז"ל, אבל להלכה הרוצה לבדוק בברכה לאור פנס רשאי, ובמקומות שיש לבודק חשש מסוים שמא להבת הנר תגרום לשרפה – עדיף שיבדוק בפנס (פסחים ז, ב; עי' שערים מצוינים בהלכה קיא, ד; יחוה דעת א, ד; סידור פסח כהלכתו יג, י).

Placing Ten Pieces of Bread

One of the interesting questions dealt with by the *poskim* concerning the procedure of *bedikat chametz* is how one can recite a *beracha* on *bedikat chametz*. Since the *beracha* is recited on the burning, *al bi'ur chametz*, as has been explained, what happens if one does not find any *chametz*? In that case, the *beracha* will have been in vain (*beracha levatala*).

The **Kol Bo** suggests that for this reason, it is customary for other family members to hide ten small pieces of bread for the one searching for *chametz* to find, thus ensuring that there will be *chametz* to burn the next day, though he adds that he does not believe this is necessary, since the meaning of the *beracha* is to burn the *chametz* only if it is found.

Sefer Kol Bo, Siman 48

It is customary in some places to hide small pieces of bread in the cracks of the house so that the one searching will find them and destroy them. As if he does not find anything, there is concern for a *beracha* recited in vain. But we have not been concerned for that, since our opinion is that **when reciting the *beracha* on burning the *chametz*, [the intention is] to burn it if it is found.**

43. ספר כלבו | סימן מח

ונהגו במקצת מקומות שמטמינין פתיתין של פת בחורי הבית כדי שימצאם הבודק ויבערם שאם לא ימצא כלום חששו לברכה לבטלה, ואנו לא חששנו בזה לפי שדעתנו כשמברכין על הבעור לבער אם נמצא.

---

19. Many other *poskim* reach a similar conclusion to the *Peninei Halacha* (and the sources he quotes) here (that strictly speaking, it is perfectly permissible, but it is customary not to where there is no potential danger involved), including Rav Moshe Stern (Responsa *Be'er Moshe* 6, *Kuntres Electric* 63), *Yesodei Yeshurun* (Vol. 6, p. 338), and others cited in the *Piskei Teshuvot* (431:2) and in the Metivta Gemara *Pesachim* Vol. 1, "*Aliba D'hilcheta*" section, *Peninei Halacha* to *Pesachim* 8a. It should be noted that unfortunately there were a few tragedies in recent years associated with fires resulting from *bedikat chametz* (and unsupervised Chanukah candles). [Addition of the English editors]

The **Rema** writes that *lechatchila* (ideally), one should hide the small pieces of bread to comply with the custom mentioned in the *Kol Bo*. However, if one did not do so, the Rema holds that one may rely on the *Kol Bo's* opinion that the *beracha* is on the actual *bedika* performed, not the finding and burning of *chametz*, and the *beracha* may therefore still be recited.

Rema, Orach Chaim 432:2 | 44.רמ"א | או"ח תלב:ב

And the custom is to place small pieces of *chametz* in places where the one searching will find them so that his *beracha* will not be in vain. But if one did not place them, it does not impede [the fulfillment of the mitzva], as the intent of every person with the *beracha* is [only] to burn if it is found.

ונוהגים להניח פתיתי חמץ במקום שימצאם הבודק, כדי שלא יהא ברכתו לבטלה. ומיהו אם לא נתן לא עכב, דדעת כל אדם עם הברכה לבער אם נמצא.

The common custom today is to place ten pieces of *chametz* out, and the **Mishna Berura** writes that there is an allusion to this custom in the writings of the **Arizal**.

Mishna Berura, Orach Chaim 432:13 | 45.משנה ברורה | או"ח תלב:יג

See the *Chok Yaakov* who writes that nevertheless [despite the fact that many hold it is not necessary to place pieces of bread out], it is not proper to abolish a custom of the Jewish people; see there where he offers reasons for the custom, **and the Arizal also writes about this custom that one should place ten small pieces out. But one should be exceedingly careful not to lose any of the pieces**...

ועיין בחק יעקב שכתב דמכל מקום אין כדאי לבטל מנהג של ישראל ועיין שם שנתן טעמים להמנהג וגם האר"י ז"ל כתב מנהג זה ושיניח יו"ד פתיתים אכן יש ליזהר הרבה שלא יאבד אחד מן הפתיתין...

It is a good idea to write down where one places the pieces in case one forgets where they are. But if nonetheless one of them gets lost, the **Ohr L'tzion** writes that one need not spend effort to find it. Rather, one should simply rely on the *bitul* performed shortly after the *bedika*.

Responsa Ohr L'tzion 3:7:17 | 46.שו"ת אור לציון | ג:ז:יז

Question: One who hid ten small pieces for the *bedikat chametz* and only found nine – what should he do?

Answer: He should search for it and [try to] find it, but if he does not find it, he may rely on the *bitul* and that suffices.

שאלה: מי שהצניע עשרה פתיתים בבדיקת חמץ, ולא מצא אלא תשעה כיצד ינהג.

תשובה: יש לו לחפשו ולמצאו, ואם לא מצא, יסמוך על הביטול שיאמר ודיו.

BITUL CHAMETZ

As mentioned above, we nullify the *chametz* right after performing the *bedika* on the night of the fourteenth. The source of this practice of *bitul* can be found in the **Gemara** in ***Pesachim.***

Masechet Pesachim 6b

Rav Yehuda said that **Rav said: One who searches** for leaven **must render** all his leaven **null and void,** cognitively and verbally. The Gemara asks: **What is the reason** for this? **If you say it is due to crumbs** that he failed to detect in his search, **they are** inherently **insignificant,** and null and void by definition…

Rava said: The reason for the requirement to render leaven null and void is based on **a decree lest he find a fine cake [*geluska*]** among the leaven that he did not destroy **and his thoughts are upon it.** Due to its significance, he will hesitate before removing it and will be in violation of the prohibition against owning leaven.

The Gemara asks: **And let him nullify it when he finds it.** The Gemara rejects this suggestion. **Perhaps he will find it** only **after it is** already **forbidden,** and at that time **it is no** longer **in his possession and he is** therefore **unable to nullify** leaven when it is already Passover, **as Rabbi Elazar said: Two items are not in a person's possession** in terms of legal ownership, **and yet the Torah rendered** him responsible for **them as though** they were **in his property. And these are they: An** open **pit in the public domain,** for which the one who excavated it is liable to pay any damages it causes even though it does not belong to him; **and leaven** in one's house **from the sixth hour** on the fourteenth of Nissan **and onward.** As this leaven has no monetary value, since it is prohibited to eat or to derive benefit from it, it is not his property, and nevertheless he violates a prohibition if it remains in his domain.

47. מסכת פסחים ו:

אמר רב יהודה אמר רב: הבודק צריך שיבטל. מאי טעמא? אי נימא משום פירורין הא לא חשיבי...

אמר רבא: גזירה שמא ימצא גלוסקא יפה ודעתיה עילויה.

וכי משכחת ליה לבטליה! – דילמא משכחת ליה לבתר איסורא, ולאו ברשותיה קיימא, ולא מצי מבטיל. דאמר רבי אלעזר: שני דברים אינן ברשותו של אדם ועשאן הכתוב כאילו ברשותו, ואלו הן: בור ברשות הרבים, וחמץ משש שעות ולמעלה.

According to the Gemara, the purpose of *bitul* is to ensure that any *chametz* that was not discovered during the *bedika* but was found later on is already rendered worthless before Pesach begins, as after that one can no longer do so.

What exactly is the meaning of the *bitul*? The literal translation of the word in English is "nullification," but what is the exact meaning of this concept? This question is subject to a dispute among the *Rishonim.* According to **Rashi,** *bitul* means mentally deciding that the *chametz* is worthless.

Rashi, Pesachim 4b

Nullification alone – As it is written, "You shall remove," and it is not written: You shall destroy, and removal in the heart is considered removal.

48. רש"י | פסחים ד:

בביטול בעלמא – דכתיב תשביתו ולא כתיב תבערו, והשבתה דלב היא השבתה.

Thus, according to Rashi, the Torah has created a novel halachic principle here that one may simply mentally declare that the *chametz* is worthless, and it then indeed takes effect. According to **Tosafot,** though, *bitul* is a form of *hefker,* rendering an object ownerless.

 Tosafot, Pesachim 4b | **.49 תוספות | פסחים ד:**

And the Ri says that by Torah law, *bitul* alone is sufficient, for the reason that since one has nullified it, it is ownerless and it has left his possession, and it is permitted, as we say: "But you may see what belongs to others [i.e., gentiles] and to God.

ואומר ר"י דמדאורייתא בביטול בעלמא סגי מטעם דמאחר שביטלו הוי הפקר ויצא מרשותו ומותר מדקאמרינן אבל אתה רואה של אחרים ושל גבוה.

In addition to the *bitul* declaration recited at night following the *bedika,* a second one is also recited on the morning of the fourteenth at the time of the burning of the *chametz,* as described in the **Shulchan Aruch.**

א **Shulchan Aruch, Orach Chaim 434:2** | **.50 שולחן ערוך | או"ח תלד:ב**

After the *bedika* at night, one immediately nullifies it and states: All *chametz* that is in my possession, that I have not seen, and that I have not burned, should be nullified, and should be like the dust of the earth. **And it is proper to nullify it again another time on the day of the fourteenth at the end of the fifth hour,** before the sixth hour arrives, as when the sixth hour arrives, it [the *chametz*] is forbidden, and one cannot nullify it.

אחר הבדיקה מיד בלילה יבטלנו ויאמר: "כל חמירא דאיתיה ברשותי דלא חזיתיה ודלא ביערתיה לבטיל וליהוי כעפרא דארעא". וטוב לחזור ולבטלו פעם אחרת ביום י"ד **סוף שעה חמישית,** קודם שתגיע שעה ששית, שמשתגיע שעה ששית נאסר ואין בידו לבטלו.

The **Rema** then adds that one should recite the *bitul* only after burning the *chametz.*

א **Rema, Orach Chaim 434:2** | **.51 רמ"א | או"ח תלד:ב**

But one should only nullify it during the day after he has burned the *chametz,* in order to fulfill the mitzva of burning with *chametz* that belongs to him [as after the *bitul,* it is no longer his].

ואין לבטלו ביום אלא לאחר ששרף החמץ, כדי לקיים מצות שריפה בחמץ שלו.

What is the reason why we perform the *bitul* twice? Wouldn't doing so once be enough? **Rav Eliezer Melamed** explains the answer in the *Peninei Halacha.*

Peninei Halacha, Pesach p. 59 | **.52 פניני הלכה | פסח עמ' 59**

And although one has already nullified the *chametz* on the night of the fourteenth after the *bedika,* nevertheless, that *bitul* was for *chametz* about which one was not aware and was not found during the *bedika.* But the *chametz* that one intends to eat at dinner one cannot nullify [yet], since it is important to us. Likewise, the *chametz* that was found during the *bedika* we do not nullify, as we intend to remove it through burning...

ואף שכבר ביטלו את החמץ בליל י"ד אחר הבדיקה, מכל מקום אותו הביטול היה על החמץ שלא נודע ולא נמצא בבדיקה. אבל את החמץ שמתכוונים לאכול בארוחות הערב – לא ניתן לבטל, מפני שהוא חשוב לנו וכן את החמץ שנמצא בבדיקה לא מבטלים שהרי מתכוונים להשביתו בשריפה...

Therefore, at night we nullify only the *chametz* that we did not find during the *bedika*, but we do not intend to nullify the *chametz* that we are keeping for the other meals and for the burning of *chametz*. Therefore, it is possible that some of this *chametz* slipped away from our eyes and was forgotten about, so in order not to violate *bal yirea'eh* and *bal yimatzei*, we nullify the *chametz* again.

לפיכך בלילה אנו מבטלים רק את החמץ שלא מצאנו בבדיקה, אבל אין אנו מתכוונים לבטל את החמץ שאנו שומרים עבור הארוחות הנותרות ושריפת החמץ. לפיכך, יתכן שמקצת מן החמץ הזה נשמט מעינינו ונשכח, וכדי שלא נעבור עליו באיסור בל יראה ובל ימצא, חוזרים ומבטלים את החמץ.

Although as we mentioned earlier in the *shiur*, according to the Torah either *bitul* or burning the *chametz* alone suffices, and it is not necessary to do both, the **Mishna Berura** explains that Chazal required performing both.

| א | **Mishna Berura, Orach Chaim 431:2** | **53. משנה ברורה | או"ח תלא:ב** |

...One also needs to nullify the *chametz* at that time, as stated later in 434:2. **And according to the Torah, one of them is sufficient,** as when one nullifies it in his heart and renders it ownerless, it is no longer his and he does not transgress [the prohibition], and certainly when he searches and looks for it and destroys it from the world. **But Chazal were stringent that one is not enough; rather both of them** [are necessary], because they were concerned since *bitul* is dependent upon the thoughts of people and their opinions, perhaps the person will be unhappy that he has *chametz* worth a few thousand to render ownerless. And even though he will declare verbally that it should be nullified and ownerless and considered like dirt, nevertheless, **this is not what he thinks in his heart,** and he will not nullify it with a complete heart, and he will thereby violate *bal yera'eh*, since he did not remove it from his house.

Moreover, **perhaps because people are used to having it all year, if it is in his house and his possession, we decree [to search for it lest] he forget and come to eat it.** Therefore, Chazal enacted that even though nullifying it is not adequate, but one must search [for it] in order to destroy it from the world, even so one must also nullify it, as perhaps one will not search properly and one will find *chametz* on Pesach and transgress on it [the prohibition].

...וגם צריך לבטל אז את החמץ וכדלקמן בסימן תל"ד סעיף ב. **ומן התורה באחד מהן סגי,** דכשמבטלו בלבו ומפקירו שוב אינו שלו ואינו עובר עליו, וכל שכן כשבודקו ומחפש אחריו ומבערו מן העולם, **אלא שחז"ל החמירו דלא סגי באחד מהן אלא בשניהם דוקא,** לפי שחששו אחר שהבטול תלוי במחשבתן של בני אדם ובדעותיהן אולי ירע בעיני האדם שיש לו חמץ בעד כמה אלפים להפקיר, ואף שבפיו יאמר שיהיה בטל והפקר וחשיב כעפרא, מכל מקום **לבו לא כן יחשוב** ולא יבטלנו בלב שלם, והרי הוא עובר ב"בל יראה", שהרי לא הוציא מביתו.

ועוד, שמא מתוך שרגילין בו כל השנה אם יהיה בביתו ורשותו גזרינן שישכח ויבוא לאכול, ולכן תקנו חז"ל שאע"פ שמבטל לא סגי, אלא צריך לבדוק לבערו מן העולם, ומכל מקום צריך לבטל גם כן, שמא לא יבדוק יפה וימצא חמץ בפסח ויעבור עליו.

Thus, we must perform *bedika* in case one's *bitul* is not sincere and to ensure one does not mistakenly eat *chametz* in one's house on Pesach, and we must also perform *bitul* in case the *bedika* is not performed fully and one finds *chametz* on Pesach.

BI'UR CHAMETZ AND FINDING CHAMETZ ON PESACH

Bi'ur Chametz

We have learned already that the *bedikat chametz* is the first step of the mitzva of *bi'ur chametz*, destroying the *chametz*. As we saw, this is the reason why the text of the *beracha* on the *bedikat chametz* is *al bi'ur chametz*. What exactly does the mitzva of *bi'ur chametz* entail? The **Mishna** in **Pesachim** records a dispute as to whether one must specifically burn the *chametz* (since the word *bi'ur* often means to burn) or whether one must destroy or dispose of it in any manner.[20]

Masechet Pesachim 21b

Rabbi Yehuda says: The removal of leavened bread is to be accomplished **only** through **burning. And the Rabbis say:** Burning is not required, as **one** may **even crumble** it **and throw** it **into the wind or cast** it **into the sea.**

54. מסכת פסחים כא:

רבי יהודה אומר אין ביעור חמץ אלא שריפה וחכמים אומרים אף מפרר וזורה לרוח או מטיל לים.

Which opinion does the halacha follow? The **Shulchan Aruch** appears to accept the opinion of the *Chachamim* that one may dispose of it in any form, but the **Rema** states that the custom is to burn it, and the **Mishna Berura** explains that the reason is to comply with those who rule that the halacha is like Rabbi Yehuda.

Shulchan Aruch, Orach Chaim 445:1

How is *bi'ur chametz* [performed]? One burns it or crushes it or throws it to the wind or throws it to the sea. And if the *chametz* is hard and the sea will not cut it up quickly, one should crush it and then throw it into the sea.

Rema: But the custom is to burn it, and it is best to burn it during the day [of the fourteenth] similar to *notar* (leftover meat from a *korban* that was burnt), which was burnt during the day. But if one wishes to burn it immediately following the search so that a weasel does not drag it away, he has the right to do so.

55. שולחן ערוך | או"ח תמה:א

כיצד ביעור חמץ? שורפו או פוררו וזורה לרוח או זורקו לים, ואם היה החמץ קשה ואין הים מחתכו במהרה – הרי זה מפררו ואחר כך זורקו לים.

הגה: והמנהג לשרופו, וטוב לשורפו ביום דומיא דנותר שהיה נשרף ביום, אך אם רצה לשורפו מיד אחר הבדיקה כדי שלא יגררנו חולדה – הרשות בידו.

---

20. Nowadays, it has become common to sell one's *chametz* to a gentile, which is another method of preventing ownership of the *chametz* over Pesach (but which is beyond the purview of this *shiur* to discuss). The mitzva of *bi'ur* should take place with *chametz* that one does not plan on selling to a gentile. [Addition of the English editors]

א Mishna Berura , Orach Chaim 445:6 | ‎56. משנה ברורה | או"ח תמה:ו

But the custom is to burn it – Since we consider the opinion of those *poskim* who rule in accordance with the opinion of Rabbi Yehuda who says that *bi'ur chametz* must be through burning, since we derive it from *notar* that is through burning…

והמנהג לשורפו – דחוששין לדעת הפוסקים שפסקו כר' יהודה דאמר אין ביעור חמץ אלא שריפה דילפינן מנותר שהוא בשריפה....

The **Mishna Berura** also details the proper time for burning the *chametz* on Erev Pesach as being prior to the sixth hour, since after that time, one is prohibited to benefit from the *chametz* and it is no longer in one's possession halachically (as the Gemara cited earlier states).

א Mishna Berura , Orach Chaim 445:7 | ‎57. משנה ברורה | או"ח תמה:ז

And it is good to burn it during the day – And the Maharil offered another reason why it is better to burn it during the day so that one will thereby remember to recite the second declaration of *bitul* that we do during the day. And we burn it during [i.e., no later than] the fifth hour [of the halachic hours of the day] since one must nullify it afterwards, and in the sixth hour, it is no longer in his possession to nullify it. If one has *hoshanot*, it is good to burn the *chametz* with the *hoshanot*, since it was used for one mitzva [the *arba minim* on Sukkot], it should be used as well for the mitzva of destroying [the *chametz*].

וטוב לשורפו ביום – ומהרי"ל כתב טעם אחר דנכון יותר לשרוף ביום כדי שמתוך זה יזכור לבטל בטול שני שמבטלין ביום. ושורפין בשעה חמישית שהרי צריך לבטל אח"כ ובשש שהוא לאו ברשותיה לבטלו [מ"א לעיל בסי' תל"ד] אם יש לו הושענות טוב לשרוף החמץ בהושענות הואיל ואיתעביד בו מצוה חדא ליתעביד בו גם מצות תשביתו.

Finding *Chametz* on Pesach

Even after one has cleaned and searched every part of the house for *chametz*, it sometimes happens that a piece of cracker or cereal is sometimes found somewhere in the house on Pesach. What should one do with the piece of *chametz*? The answer is that it depends on whether the *chametz* is discovered on Yom Tov/Shabbat or on the weekdays of *Chol HaMo'ed* (the intermediate days). The **Gemara** in *Pesachim* states that if one finds *chametz* on Yom Tov, one should cover it.

ח Masechet Pesachim 6a | ‎58. מסכת פסחים ו.

Rav Yehuda said that **Rav said: One who finds leavened bread in his house on the Festival,** i.e., the first day of Pesach, **covers it with a vessel** and burns it at the conclusion of the Festival day.

אמר רב יהודה אמר רב: המוצא חמץ בביתו ביום טוב – כופה עליו את הכלי.

Rashi explains that the reason for this is that the *chametz* is *muktzeh* and may not be moved on Yom Tov or Shabbat. Therefore, to ensure that one does not come to eat it, one covers it until after Yom Tov or Shabbat.

Rashi, Pesachim 6a

Covers it with a vessel – Because it is not suitable for moving and removing. However, he has not violated *bal yera'eh* since he nullified it in his heart yesterday [i.e., on *Erev Pesach*], as we say below: One who searches must nullify it in his heart. Rather, turning over a utensil is required so that he does not forget and eat it.

59. רש"י | פסחים ו.

כופה עליו את הכלי – דהא לא חזי לטלטולי ואפוקי, ומיהו, ב"בל יראה" לא עבר, דהא בטליה בליביה מאתמול, כדאמרינן לקמן: הבודק צריך שיבטל בלבו, אלא משום שלא ישכח ויאכלנו – צריך כפיית כלי.

The **Shulchan Aruch** rules this way as well.

Shulchan Aruch, Orach Chaim 446:1

One who finds *chametz* in his house [should do as follows]: **If it is on *Chol HaMo'ed*, he should remove it and burn it immediately. And if it is Yom Tov, one should place a utensil on it until nighttime and then burn it,** since he may not move it on Yom Tov. It is also forbidden to burn it in its place.[21]

60. שולחן ערוך | או"ח תמו:א

המוצא חמץ בביתו, אם הוא בחול המועד – יוציאנו ויבערנו מיד. ואם הוא יום טוב – **יכפה** עליו כלי עד הלילה ואז יבערנו לפי שלא יוכל לטלטלו ביום טוב, גם לשרפו במקומו אסור.

Rav Shmuel Vozner writes though that nowadays the halacha is different. Since today everyone sells their *chametz* to a gentile, any *chametz* found on Pesach actually belongs to that gentile. Therefore, one may not burn or dispose of it.

Responsa Shevet HaLevi 9:116

If the *chametz* was indeed sold, then it [the *chametz* found] has the status of *chametz* owned by a gentile that is found in the property of a Jew without him accepting responsibility for it, for which on Yom Tov one should place a utensil on top of it, as explained in *siman* 446. And on *Chol HaMo'ed* one should make a separation of ten [handbreadths].[22]

61. שו"ת שבט הלוי | ט:קטז

אם חמץ זה באמת מכור, אם כן דינו כחמץ של גוי הנמצא ברשות ישראל בלי קבלת אחריות שביום טוב כופה עליו כלי כמבואר סי' תמ"ו ובחול המועד עושה מחיצה יו"ד.

The halacha is also different if one finds *chametz* in the street or other public area (even in Israel). In that case, one should not touch it for any reason, as the moment that one picks it up, he acquires it and thereby violates the prohibition of *bal yera'eh*. This is explained by the **Bi'ur Halacha** citing the **Rivash**.

---

21. Although using fire on Yom Tov is permitted and one has not moved it in this case, it must serve some purpose related to the Yom Tov itself, while the burning is not related to some need or enjoyment for the Yom Tov (*Mishna Berura* 446:6). [Addition of the English editors]

22. This is the conclusion of Rav Tzvi Pesach Frank as well (*Mikra'ei Kodesh*, Pesach 1:74), though he allows placing the *chametz* with the rest of the items sold to the gentile rather than requiring the erection of a separation around the location of the *chametz* found. The *Piskei Teshuvot* (446, footnote 7) notes though that for those who do not rely on the sale of *chametz* for actual *chametz*, the custom today is still to burn or dispose of actual *chametz* in the same manner as described in the classical sources. [Addition of the English editors]

א Bi'ur Halacha, Orach Chaim Siman 446

62. ביאור הלכה | או"ח סימן תמו

In his house – Rav Yitzchak ben Sheshet [Rivash] writes: **If one finds *chametz* in the public domain, it is forbidden for him to pick it up, as one acquires it the moment one picks it up and violates *bal yera'eh*.** And even if one's intention is not to acquire it, but rather he raises it up in order to remove it from a place where the public passes it so that they should not stumble over it, it is also forbidden…

בביתו – כתב הרב יצחק בן ששת בסימן ת"א: **מצא חמץ ברשות הרבים – אסור לו להגביהו, דמשעה שהגביהו קנאו ועובר עליו ב"בל יראה".** ואפילו אין דעתו לזכות בו, אלא מגביהו כדי לסלקו ממקום שרבים עוברים עליו כדי שלא יכשלו בו – נמי אסור...

FURTHER IYUN

For further *iyun* concerning *mechirat chametz* (the sale of *chametz*), see page 48.

SUMMARY OF THE LAWS OF
BEDIKAT, BITUL AND BI'UR CHAMETZ

Studying the Laws of Pesach

1. **Gemara *Pesachim*** – One inquires about and expounds (*sho'alin v'dorshin*) the laws of Pesach beginning thirty days before the holiday.

2. **Gemara *Megilla*** – One studies the laws of the holiday on the holiday itself.

3. **Ran/Rav Ovadia Yosef** – The obligation is to study the halachot on the holiday itself, and the Gemara *Pesachim* simply means that within thirty days, one who asks a question about the holiday is responded to first.

4. **Tosafot/*Bi'ur Halacha*** – One must study the halachot thirty days before based on the Gemara in *Pesachim*, and the study on the holiday refers to providing the philosophical reasons behind the observing of the holiday.

What Is the Reason for Bedikat Chametz?

1. **Mishna *Pesachim*** – We search for *chametz* on the night of the fourteenth.

2. **Rashi** – The purpose is to prevent one from violating the prohibition of *bal yera'eh*, not owning *chametz* on Pesach.

3. **Tosafot** – The purpose is to ensure that one does not come to find it on Yom Tov and eat it.

4. **Ran** – Explains Rashi's opinion that even though *bitul* is sufficient, we search as well in case some people do not recite the *bitul* honestly.

The Time for Bedikat Chametz and the Accompanying Restrictions

1. **Gemara *Pesachim*** – *Bedika* is done at night because that is when people are home plus using a candle is more effective at night.

2. **Ra'avad/*Shulchan Aruch*/*Mishna Berura*** – The proper time is immediately after nightfall.

3. **Gemara *Pesachim*/*Shulchan Aruch*** – Therefore, one should not engage in activities and eating a meal close to that time. Torah study also should not be begun at that time. There is a *machloket Acharonim* if Torah study is forbidden during the half-hour before.

4. *Magen Avraham/Yalkut Yosef* – A set Torah study group or shiur is permitted because they will remind each other to perform *bedikat chametz*.

5. *Mishna Berura/Yalkut Yosef* – A *k'beitza* of bread or grain is forbidden to eat beforehand.

6. *Ohr L'tzion* – One who works late and wishes to remain in his store may appoint an agent to perform the *bedika* in his home, though it is preferred for him to do so himself.

Where Must Bedikat Chametz Be Performed?

1. Every room in the house into which *chametz* is brought must be searched. This also includes the car.

2. *Mishna Berura* – Shuls also must be searched, and a *beracha* may be recited, though some disagree.

3. **Must *sefarim* be searched for *chametz*?**
   a. *Chazon Ish*/**Rav Mordechai Eliyahu** – Yes
   b. **Rav Ovadia Yosef** – No

The Procedure for Bedikat Chametz

1. *Gemara Pesachim* – There is a dispute as to the correct text of the *beracha,* our practice is to recite *al bi'ur chametz*.

2. *Mishna Berura* – We refer to the *bedika* in the *beracha* and not the *bi'ur* this is the beginning of the mitzva of *bi'ur*, plus it cannot be recited on the *bitul*, since that depends upon one's mindset.

3. **May one use a flashlight?**
   a. **Gemara Pesachim** – Derives from *pesukim* that one uses a candle, but gives a number of reasons for it (it searches well in cracks, it is less dangerous than a torch, etc.), all of which are applicable to a flashlight as well.
   b. *Peninei Halacha* – The halacha is that one may use a flashlight, but many maintain the custom of using a candle except for where it is dangerous.

4. **Placing Pieces of Bread**
   a. *Kol Bo* – It is customary to place pieces of bread around the house to ensure that *chametz* is found and the *beracha* recited (on burning the *chametz*) is not in vain.
   b. **Arizal** – There are Kabbalistic reasons for placing ten pieces of bread out.

    i.   If one did not place any pieces out, the *beracha* is not invalid and is on the act of searching.

    ii. If one forgot where the pieces of bread were hidden, one may rely on the *bitul* performed that the bread has been nullified. Ideally one should write down where the pieces were placed so they do not get lost.

Bitul Chametz

1. Following the *bedika,* one should recite the declaration of *kol chami'a* that nullifies the *chametz.*

2. **Shulchan Aruch** – It is customary to nullify the *chametz* once at night and once the next day.

3. **What is the essence of the *bitul*?**

    a. **Rashi** – It is mentally rendering it worthless.

    b. **Tosafot** – It is rendering it ownerless.

4. *Mishna Berura* – We perform both *bedika* and *bitul* to ensure that one does not recite the *bitul* insincerely but also that if one missed *chametz* in his search that it is still rendered worthless.

Bi'ur Chametz and Finding Chametz on Pesach

1. **Mishna** – Brings a *machloket* whether *bi'ur chametz* is only through burning or any means of disposal.

2. **Shulchan Aruch/Rema** – One may dispose of *chametz* in any manner, but the custom is to burn it.

3. *Mishna Berura* – The burning should take place no later than the fifth hour.

4. **Gemara** – One who finds *chametz* on Yom Tov in his property should place a utensil on top of it and proceed to burn it on *Chol HaMo'ed.*

5. *Shevet HaLevi* – Nowadays when everyone sells their *chametz,* if it is found on Pesach, it belongs to the gentile who bought the *chametz,* and one should make a separation of ten *tefachim* around it.

6. *Bi'ur Halacha* – If one finds *chametz* in public one should not pick it up, as one thereby acquires the *chametz* and one violates the prohibition of *bal yera'eh.*

FURTHER IYUN

Mechirat Chametz – A Halachic and Historic Overview

Rav Joel Kenigsberg (Graduate, the Manhigut Toranit program)

Anyone who has experienced the arduous days of cleaning leading up to Pesach is well aware that the Torah's prohibition of *chametz* is like no other. Even the smallest crumb is forbidden for consumption, and alongside the ban on eating and deriving benefit, the mitzvot of *bal yeira'eh* and *bal yimatzei* dictate that no *chametz* may enter our possession.

The custom of *mechirat chametz* (along with *bedika*, *biur* and *bittul*) was established as a safeguard in order to prevent two possible problems:

1. Transgressing the **biblical** prohibitions of *bal yeira'eh* and *bal yimatzei*.
2. Allowing the *chametz* for use after Pesach and prevention of the **rabbinic** penalty of *chametz she'avar alav haPesach*.

While burning seems like a fully understandable method of eliminating one's *chametz*, the custom of selling it to a non-Jew raises many questions. How can it be considered a serious sale when the buyer and seller never come into contact, and it is clear to all that the *chametz* will return to the possession of its original owners at the conclusion of the *chag*? Furthermore, the fact that the *chametz* never leaves the Jew's home only compounds the halachic difficulties in performing such a sale.

In order to understand better just how and why this sale works, it is helpful to go back and explore its historic origins.

The Origins of *Mechirat Chametz*

Rav Shlomo Yosef Zevin, in his *HaMoadim B'halacha*, traces the development of the custom of *mechirat chametz* through four historical periods:

The earliest mention of the idea of selling *chametz* to a non-Jew is found in the **Mishna:**[1] "During the hour that one may eat *chametz* he may feed it to animals and birds or sell it a non-Jew". The **Gemara** explains that the Mishna comes to support the opinion of Beit Hillel that this sale is permitted even close to the onset of Pesach, when it is clear that the *chametz* will not be consumed before the *chag*. What emerges clearly from the Mishna and Gemara is the description of a regular transaction like any other between buyer and seller.[2]

During the next stage, the sale retained its authentic form in that the non-Jewish buyer received his merchandise and the Jewish seller received his payment. However, both were

---

1. *Pesachim* 21a.
2. See also *Pesachim* 13a for a description of the sale of *chametz* in a similar context.

aware that the *chametz* would be repurchased by the Jew at the conclusion of the *chag*. The **Tosefta**[3] brings the case of a Jew and a non-Jew who are together on a ship on *Erev Pesach* and allows for the Jew to sell his *chametz* to the non-Jew even when he plans to repurchase it after Pesach (so long as he performs a valid sale). Seemingly, this model is the basis for the halacha in the **Shulchan Aruch** which sanctions the sale of *chametz* to a non-Jew.[4] Nonetheless, the impression formed by the Tosefta is of a spontaneous sale on a case by case basis, far from the pre-organized ritual that exists today.

Several hundred years ago the sale began to take on a more formal and even disingenuous appearance. Many of the Jews of Europe earned their livelihood through the manufacture of alcoholic beverages such as whiskey which constitute *chametz*. In addition, the *chametz* not used in the manufacture of the beverages would be used to feed their animals. The disposal of the *chametz* before Pesach would entail great monetary loss, and so the prearranged sale of *chametz* began to take shape. The *chametz* would remain in the home of the Jew, and the non-Jew's ownership of it became more of a legal technicality than a tangible reality. In order to downplay the somewhat fictitious appearance and strengthen the authenticity of the sale, the signing of a document of sale became an integral part of the process as well. The sale was performed on an individual basis by members of the community.

The complex nature of the sale described above (whereby the sold *chametz* remained in the home of the seller) led to a large number of cases where its halachic validity was called into question. Cases are recorded whereby the seller forgot to sign his name on the document or where the *chametz* was sold after the time when it had already become forbidden. The fact that many of those executing the sale were ignorant of the relevant halachot meant that while they thought they had sold their *chametz*, it remained fully in their possession. As a result, the practice which continues to this day was established: the local *beit din* would arrange a collective sale for all members of the community. Originally this sale took on the form of a collective sale of *chametz* to the Rav, who would then sell it to the non-Jew. Later this was changed to our current practice whereby the Rav does not himself purchase the *chametz*, but rather acts as an agent for the sale of the *chametz* belonging to the members of the community to the non-Jew.

Controversy of the Sale

Despite its widespread nature, the evolution of the sale into the form in which it exists today was not without controversy. The sale was, and remains seen by many, as a deliberate form of deception (*ha'arama* in halachic terminology). The **Bechor Shor** writes that *mechirat chametz* is undoubtedly to be considered *ha'arama* since the buyer never really intended to provide payment or purchase his goods, and the seller too never seriously planned to give up ownership. Consequently, the sale would be ineffective regarding the biblical prohibition of *chametz*.[5]

The *Bechor Shor* writes that the sale is nonetheless valid under certain circumstances, since

---

3. Brought by the *Beit Yosef*, O.C. 448.

4. *Shulchan Aruch*, O.C. 448:3.

5. A full treatment of the topic of *ha'arama* is beyond the scope of this essay. The validity of this mechanism is subject to a dispute among the *Rishonim* and the view of the *Bechor Shor* is that *ha'arama* is a valid mechanism only to overcome transgressions of rabbinic origin.

after performing *bittul*, the prohibition of *chametz* is only rabbinic in nature. Yet this approach raises even more questions. If the *bittul* is to be taken seriously how can one sell that which he has already nullified and is considered as dust of the earth? And if the *bittul* is meant to be done after the sale, if the sale is to be taken seriously, how can one affect the legal status of that which is not in his possession?[6]

The *Bechor Shor*, as a leading halachic authority of his day could not be taken lightly. However, his opinion was ultimately rejected by most *poskim*.[7] Some argued that since the sold *chametz* was by definition excluded from the *bittul*, any *mechirat chametz* would be coming to prevent a biblical transgression. Others claimed that *mechirat chametz* is not to be considered *ha'arama* at all. Since theoretically the non-Jew could complete his payment and take up ownership of his newly bought goods, so long as the buyer and seller genuinely agree on the sale, and all other technical aspects are done properly, there is no reason not to consider the sale authentically binding.[8]

Outside of the House

As mentioned above, the contrived nature of the sale stems in no small part from the fact that the *chametz* never leaves the home of the Jew. In fact, the **Shulchan Aruch**[9] writes that one's *chametz* may be sold to a non-Jew specifically on condition that it is removed from the Jew's home. Exploring the rationale behind this condition can lend some insight into how today's sale is nonetheless considered valid.

Selling the House Along with the *Chametz*

Several approaches are offered by the *Acharonim* to explain the requirement to remove the *chametz* from the Jew's home. Ordinarily there is no prohibition against the presence of *chametz* belonging to a non-Jew in the home of a Jew, so long as two conditions are met:

a. A partition should be established lest the Jew accidentally come to eat from the *chametz*.[10]

b. The Jew may bear no monetary responsibility for the *chametz* in the event that it becomes lost or stolen.[11]

Nonetheless, the case of *mechirat chametz* is different since the *chametz* belonged to the Jew to begin with and hence there is more reason for concern. The **Bach** writes that leaving the *chametz* in place makes it appear as if the Jew received a deposit of *chametz* from the non-Jew, accompanied by monetary liability.

The *Bach* does provide a solution for situations where it would be impractical to remove the *chametz*, such as where the quantity is too large. Rather than removing the *chametz* itself, the room which contains the *chametz* may be sold to the non-Jew, along with its contents. In order for the sale of the room to be effective the key would also have to be transferred to the non-Jew. Alternatively, writes the **Mishna Berura**, it should be explicitly stated that the non-Jewish buyer may approach the Jewish seller at any time to receive the key in order to access his *chametz*. Indeed, in the sale performed today in many communities,

---

6. See Responsa *Chatam Sofer*, o.c. 62.

7. See Responsa *Oneg Yom Tov* 28, *Mekor Chaim*, o.c. 8, *Sedei Chemed*, *Chametz U'matza* 9:3.

8. See Rav Moshe Shternbuch's *Teshuvot V'Hanhagot* 5:112 for an alternative explanation in rejection of the *Bechor Shor*'s approach. It should be noted, though, that Rav Shternbuch questions the validity of the sale on other grounds.

9. o.c. 448:3.

10. *Pesachim* 6a and *Shulchan Aruch*, o.c. 440:2.

11. *Shulchan Aruch*, ibid.

such a condition is written into the document of sale. In order for the sale to be taken seriously, it would seem fitting that the Jew selling his *chametz* should be aware of this condition.[12]

This solution itself is not without its problems, however. A dispute exists among the *Acharonim* as to whether the location of the *chametz* should be sold or leased.[13] According to the **Mekor Chaim**, a sale is necessary to avoid transgressing the biblical prohibitions of *bal yeira'eh* and *bal yimatzei*. However, the **Noda BiYehuda** and **Chatam Sofer** write quite the opposite. They prefer leasing rather than an outright sale as this seems more authentic.[14]

Ma'aseh Kinyan[15]

The *Chok Ya'akov* explains the necessity of removing the *chametz* from the Jew's home as a technical rather than an intrinsic requirement. Removing the *chametz* and bringing it to the buyer would allow *meshicha* to be performed as *a ma'aseh kinyan*.

Accordingly, if another valid means of performing the *kinyan* could be found, there would no problem with leaving the *chametz* where it is and transferring ownership to the non-Jew. The difficulty here is that the *poskim* struggle to agree on an acceptable means of *kinyan* regarding transactions involving non-Jews. Below we provide a brief overview of some of the possible methods listed by the **Mishna Berura**,[16] as well as the questions raised by each one.[17] (The methods of *meshicha* and *hagba'a* are excluded from this discussion, since we assume that circumstances dictate that it is not possible to remove the *chametz* physically.)

The **Gemara (Bava Metzia 48b)** records a dispute between Rabbi Yochanan and Reish Lakish regarding how transfer of ownership is affected halachically. According to Reish Lakish, **meshicha** is necessary by Torah law. For Rabbi Yochanan, the transfer of **money** would suffice biblically, but Chazal established that a *ma'aseh kinyan* such as *meshicha* would be necessary as well.

The **Gemara** in **Bechorot** (13b) explains that the *machloket* between them only applies regarding transactions between Jews.[18] However, regarding transactions involving non-Jews the halacha would be reversed. Therefore, since Rabbi Yochanan rules that money suffices biblically to enact a transaction between Jews, where a non-Jew is involved it would not suffice. And since most *poskim* rule like Rabbi Yochanan, the transfer of money would not be a valid *ma'aseh kinyan*. **Rashi**, though, does rule like Reish Lakish, and so if we rely on his opinion, we could affect the sale of *chametz* through monetary payment.[19]

Other possible *kinyanim* include **chalifin**

---

12. In instances where the seller is travelling overseas for the duration of the *chag*, it may be necessary to leave a key with a neighbor or provide other contact information so that theoretically the buyer would still have access to his *chametz* should he choose to use it.

13. See *Teshuvot V'hanhagot* 5:112 for a summary of the various opinions.

14. The current practice is to lease out the location of the *chametz*. It is worth noting that those who rent their property would be unable to sell the location in any event.

15. A *ma'aseh kinyan* is a physical act which demonstrates transfer of ownership and is necessary in order for a transaction to be halachically valid. Examples include *meshicha* (pulling the object) and *hagba'a* (lifting the object).

16. *Mishna Berura* 448:17.

17. *Sha'ar HaTziun* 448:42.

18. The Gemara learns from the verse "או קנה מיד עמיתך" that the *kinyanim* being referred to are only between Jews.

19. Even without paying the entire amount for the goods in question, the sale can still be implemented. A partial payment or down payment is received from the buyer and the rest of the sum is converted into a loan.

(exchange) – whereby an object (other than the goods which are being sold) is given from the buyer to the seller in order to create the transfer of ownership, *agav* – whereby the sale of land is expanded to include the moveable objects (in this case the *chametz*) as well, and *kinyan chatzer* – whereby any objects located in the domain of the buyer are automatically acquired to him.

Yet while all of these are valid as methods of transferring ownership between Jews, it is unclear if they hold validity with non-Jews as well. The **Shach**[20] claims that *chalifin* is not a valid form of transaction regarding non-Jews. A *kinyan agav* may only be effective rabbinically and not biblically,[21] and several opinions hold that a *kinyan chatzer* is based on *shlichut* (agency),[22] a law which does not apply to non-Jews.

Another possible solution would be a **kinyan situmta** – an agreed upon method of purchase between merchants. Yet the problem here is that it is not clear if such an agreed upon method exists for the sale of *chametz*. The **Bi'ur Halacha** writes not to rely on a *kinyan situmta* alone, but rather to perform an additional *kinyan* along with it. And because of the doubts expressed by the *poskim* regarding each form of *kinyan*, whenever several *kinyanim* are performed together, it should be stated that each *kinyan* stands alone.

Modern Technology – Sales via the Internet

In recent years, the concept of authorizing a Rav to perform *mechirat chametz* on one's behalf via the internet has become more and more prevalent, raising new halachic questions. It is important to stress though that the process of sale described in the previous paragraphs is what takes place between the Rav (as representative of the community) and the non-Jewish buyer of the *chametz*. It would seem difficult to argue that the sale could be affected with a non-Jew via the internet (Trying to reconcile the long list of possible *kinyanim* above with the intricacies of modern technology is no easy feat.). Indeed, the rabbi selling the *chametz* generally finds a local non-Jew with whom it is easy to interact personally.

By contrast, when the members of the community approach the Rav to sell their *chametz*, the purpose here is not to perform the halachic transfer of ownership but rather to appoint the Rav as a *shaliach* to sell the *chametz*. The **Rambam**[23] writes that no *ma'aseh kinyan* is necessary to appoint a *shaliach*, but merely a clear statement of intention. The completion of an online form including one's name, ID number, address and contact details, surely fulfills this requirement.

Conclusions – to Rely on the Sale or Not?

As we have seen, the custom of *mechirat chametz* is not without its controversy or complications. The **Vilna Gaon** writes[24] not to perform any sale of *chametz* which the seller intends to repurchase. The appearance of *ha'arama* and the difficulty in finding a valid *ma'aseh kinyan* are two of the most significant factors which have led several of the *Acharonim* to question the validity of the practice.

As a result of these concerns, many are stringent and choose not to rely on the sale for items which are *chametz gamur*. Yet even among those

---

20. с.м. 123.
21. See *Ketzot HaChoshen*, *siman* 194.
22. Emunat Shmuel as quoted by the *Sha'ar HaTziun*.
23. *Hilchot Mechira* 5:12.
24. *Ma'aseh Rav*, Siddur HaGra 180–181.

who are stringent for themselves, many will purchase *chametz* after Pesach from those who did rely on the sale. In this context we can draw two distinctions:

1. Great monetary loss is an important consideration in deciding the halacha. So the sale of *chametz* may be improper for the individual consumer, yet acceptable for large supermarket chain.

2. The possession of *chametz* during Pesach involves the infringement of biblical prohibitions, as we have seen. By contrast, the ban on deriving benefit from *chametz* which was owned by a Jew on Pesach is a penalty of rabbinic nature and as such there is more room for leniency.[25]

The custom of *mechirat chametz* has become entrenched in Jewish communities around the world as an integral part of the preparations for Pesach, and those who rely on the sale certainly have valid halachic grounds for doing so. The custom developed not in order to replace the physical destruction of the *chametz* in our possession, but in order to help those who found themselves in a position of great monetary loss to fulfill the halacha nonetheless. With proper planning and forethought in the weeks leading up to Pesach we can ensure that we all arrive at the *chag chametz*-free.

---

25. As expressed by the *Mishna Berura* 448:17.

2

Hilchot Leil Haseder I
הלכות ליל הסדר א'

Kadesh

Urchatz

Karpas

Yachatz

Maggid

Rachtzah

Motzee-Matza

For quick reference, some long website URLs have been shortened.
For the complete list of referenced websites visit www.tzurbaolami.com.

ת	Tanach	
ת	Talmud (Chazal)	
ר	*Rishonim*	
א	*Acharonim*	
פ	Contemporary Halachic Sources	

INTRODUCTION

The Seder night is a unique annual experience whereby we not only remember the Exodus from Egypt, but also relive it. This experience is designed to strengthen our belief that Hashem protects us throughout history from those who oppress us. It also serves as an opportunity to thank Him for transforming us into His chosen people.

Due to the importance of this evening, it is quite understandable that there are numerous *halachot* associated with the different steps of the Seder, many of which we will review in these two *shiurim*.

The Seder night consists of four general sections:

1. *Kiddush* and other introductory steps
2. *Maggid* [the telling of the story of the Exodus]
3. The mitzvot of eating [*Matza, Maror, Korech, Shulchan Orech*]
4. *Hallel*

The four cups of wine divide the evening into these four sections: We make *Kiddush* on the first cup, we tell the story of the Exodus over the second cup, we drink the third cup after we have eaten, and we recite *Hallel* over the fourth cup. This division is outlined by the Rambam in the *Mishneh Torah*:

 Rambam, Hilchot Chametz Umatza 7:10

1. רמב"ם | הל' חמץ ומצה ז:י

Regarding each of the four cups, one recites a separate *beracha*. One recites *Kiddush* over the first cup, one reads the *Haggada* over the second cup, one recites *birkat hamazon* over the third cup, and one completes the *Hallel* over the fourth cup and recites *Birkat Hashir*.[1] Between these cups, if one wishes to drink [another cup of wine] one may drink; but between the third and fourth [cup] one may not drink.

כל כוס וכוס מארבעה כוסות האלו מברך עליו ברכה בפני עצמה, וכוס ראשון אומר עליו קדוש היום, כוס שני קורא עליו את ההגדה, כוס שלישי מברך עליו ברכת המזון, כוס רביעי גומר עליו את ההלל ומברך עליו ברכת השיר, ובין הכוסות האלו אם רצה לשתות שותה בין שלישי לרביעי אינו שותה.

---

1. *Birkat Hashir* refers either to the paragraph known as "*nishmat*" or the one called "*yehalelucha*" (based on the dispute in the Gemara *Pesachim* 118a), both of which are recited today following *Hallel* at the Seder. [Addition of the English editors]

KADESH

The Mitzva of Drinking Four Cups of Wine

The **Gemara** teaches that there is a rabbinic mitzva to drink four cups of wine on the Seder night.

Masechet Pesachim 108b	**2. מסכת פסחים קח:**

It was taught in a *beraita*: Everyone is obligated regarding the four cups; men, women and children.

תנו רבנן: הכל חייבין בארבעה כוסות הללו, אחד אנשים ואחד נשים, ואחד תינוקות.

The Gemara (*Pesachim* 117b) explains the reason as follows: "The four cups of wine were instituted as a manner of freedom." The **Rambam** explains this to mean that by drinking the four cups, we demonstrate that we are free people.

Rambam, Hilchot Chametz Umatza 7:6–7	**3. רמב"ם | הל' חמץ ומצה ז:ו–ז**

6. In every generation, a person is obligated to depict himself as if he himself came out of the slavery in Egypt right now, as it is stated: "And He took us out from there" (*Devarim* 6:23). Regarding this matter, the Holy One, blessed be He commanded in the Torah: "And you shall remember that you were a slave in Egypt" (*Devarim* 5:14), i.e., as if you yourself were a slave and came out to freedom and were redeemed.

7. Therefore, when one eats on this night, he must eat and drink while reclining in a manner of freedom, and everyone, whether men or women, are obligated to drink four cups of wine on this night. One may not decrease from that [amount], and they may not give even a poor person who is supported from charity less than four cups.

ו. בכל דור ודור חייב אדם להראות את עצמו כאילו הוא בעצמו יצא עתה משעבוד מצרים שנאמר "ואותנו הוציא משם" וגו' (דברים ו), ועל דבר זה צוה הקדוש ברוך הוא בתורה "וזכרת כי עבד היית" (דברים ה) – כלומר כאילו אתה בעצמך היית עבד ויצאת לחירות ונפדית.

ז. לפיכך, כשסועד אדם בלילה הזה צריך לאכול ולשתות והוא מיסב דרך חירות, וכל אחד ואחד בין אנשים בין נשים חייב לשתות בלילה הזה ארבעה כוסות של יין, אין פוחתין מהם, ואפילו עני המתפרנס מן הצדקה לא יפחתו לו מארבעה כוסות.

Since the Rambam groups the mitzva of drinking four cups together with other activities demonstrating freedom, such as reclining, it is evident that drinking a large amount of wine is another method of demonstrating our freedom, as a slave would not be permitted to drink as much as he wants. Nevertheless, the Sages instituted the practice of drinking specifically four cups of wine to correspond to the four expressions of redemption, as explained by **Rashi**.

Rashi, Pesachim 99b

The four cups – These are parallel to the four expressions of redemption that are stated regarding the exile of Egypt: "I will bring you out, and I will save you, and I will redeem you, and I will take you," as found in *Parshat Va'era* (*Shemot* 6:6–7).

4. רש"י | פסחים צט:

ארבע כוסות – כנגד ארבעה לשוני גאולה האמורים בגלות מצרים והוצאתי אתכם והצלתי אתכם וגאלתי אתכם ולקחתי אתכם בפרשת וארא.[2]

FURTHER IYUN
For a discussion on the custom of the fifth cup in halacha and *hashkafa*, see page 88.

How Much Wine Must One Drink?

With regard to a standard *kos shel beracha* (cup of wine upon which a mitzva is performed) such as *Kiddush*, one must drink a minimum amount of a *melo lugmav*, or cheek-full, defined as the amount of wine with which one can fill one side of the cheek (usually around 50–55 cc, based on the *Bi'ur Halacha, siman* 271). This is based on the Gemara's statement (*Pesachim* 107a): "One who recites *Kiddush* and drinks a cheek-full has fulfilled his obligation, but less than that he hasn't fulfilled his obligation." However, regarding the four cups of wine on the Seder night, the **Gemara** states that one must drink the majority of the cup.

Masechet Pesachim 108b

Rav Nachman Bar Yitzchak stated: And this is only where he drank the majority of the cup.

5. מסכת פסחים קח:

אמר רב נחמן בר יצחק: והוא דאשתי רובא דכסא.

The *Rishonim* dispute the meaning of this phrase. According to **Tosafot**, one need only drink a cheek-full of the four cups, just like concerning a standard *Kiddush*. The Gemara used the phrase "the majority of the cup" to refer to the majority of a *revi'it* (one-fourth of a *log*), which is actually a cheek-full (the Gemara was referring to a standard cup that holds a *revi'it*). However, even if the volume of the cup is much greater, this opinion holds that one need only drink a cheek-full.

Tosafot, Pesachim 108b

The majority of the cup – Meaning a cheek-full, as was explained earlier. However, *lechatchila* (ideally) one should drink an entire *revi'it*.

6. תוספות | פסחים קח:

רובא דכסא – היינו כמלא לוגמיו כדפרישית לעיל ומיהו לכתחילה צריך לשתות רביעית.

However, the **Ramban** and **Ra'ah** argue, explaining that the four cups are unique and one must drink the majority of the cup, even if it is a large cup, and ideally drink the entire cup if possible.

---

2. Rav Shlomo Zalman Auerbach asks: It is understandable why we drink four cups, but why must such a cup consist specifically of wine? He answers that wine is unique in that the more aged it is, the better it becomes. Similarly, during each stage of the redemption, we will achieve even greater heights than the previous one, concluding with the final stage of "I will take you to me for as a nation."

Beit Yosef, Orach Chaim Siman 472

This is the language of the *Orchot Chaim*: "The Ramban writes that one must drink the majority of any cup, even [if the volume of the cup] contains multiple measures of a *revi'it*."

7. בית יוסף | או"ח סימן תעב

זו לשון ארחות חיים (סדר ליל הפסח סי' ו) והרמב"ן כתב שצריך לשתות רוב מכל כוס אפילו מחזיק כמה רביעיות.

Bayit Chadash (Bach), Orach Chaim Siman 472

This is indicated by the language "majority of the cup," meaning that whatever is in the cup is considered the definition of "the cup," and one must always drink the majority of the cup. For the Ramban explains that drinking "a cheek-full" was only stated regarding *Kiddush* and *birkat hamazon*, as there we only require tasting [*te'ima*] of the cup, and drinking a cheek-full is considered tasting even concerning a large cup. Therefore, even *lechatchila* there is no need to drink an entire *revi'it*; rather a cheek-full is sufficient, which is equivalent to the majority of a *revi'it*. However, here where there is an obligation to drink four cups, it is not considered as if one drank a cup unless one drank the majority of that cup. Therefore, when [the Gemara] refers to the four cups it does not state the measurement of a cheek-full, but rather it states: "This is where he drank the majority of the cup," be it a small cup of a *revi'it* or a big cup. This is true *bedieved* (after the fact), but *lechatchila* one should drink the entire cup.

8. בית חדש (ב"ח) | או"ח סימן תעב

והכי משמע לישנא דרובא דכסא דקאמר דכל מה שיש בכוס הוא הכוס וצריך שישתה רוב הכוס לעולם, דהרמב"ן ז"ל מפרש דטעימת מלא לוגמיו לא קתני לה אלא אגבי קידוש וברכת המזון דהתם לא בעינן רק טעימת הכוס ובטעימת מלא לוגמיו הוי טעימה אפילו בכוס גדול והלכך אפילו לכתחלה לא בעי למיטעם רביעית שלם אלא סגי במלא לוגמיו דהיינו רוב רביעית אבל כאן דבעינן שישתה ארבע כוסות ולא הוה שתית כוס אא"כ שותה רוב הכוס ולכך לא קאמר גבי ארבע כוסות והוא דשתי מלא לוגמיו אלא קאמר והוא דשתי רובא דכסא בין כוס קטן של רביעית בין כוס גדול הרבה והיינו דוקא דיעבד אבל לכתחלה צריך לשתות כולו.

The **Bach** explains further (in the continuation of the piece quoted above) that according to the Ramban, the reason for the distinction between *Kiddush* and the four cups is that regarding *Kiddush*, the primary mitzva is the recitation of the *beracha*. Since the one reciting the *beracha* must taste some of the cup, it is sufficient to taste a cheek-full. But regarding the four cups of wine, the mitzva is to drink in a manner of freedom. Therefore, simply tasting the wine is insufficient; rather one must drink the majority of the cup, and according to the **Rosh**, *lechatchila* one must drink the entire cup.

The **Shulchan Aruch** codifies the opinion of Tosafot that drinking the majority of a *revi'it* is sufficient as the normative halacha. He then mentions the opinion of the Ramban that one must drink the majority of the cup, even if it is a large cup.

Shulchan Aruch, Orach Chaim 472:9

The cup must contain a *revi'it* [of wine] after it is diluted (if one wants to dilute it), and one must drink the entire cup or the majority of it. If the cup contains many amounts of a *revi'it*, many people can drink from the cup according to the number of measures of *revi'it* in it. And some say that one has to drink the majority of the cup even if it contains many measures of a *revi'it* in it.

9. שולחן ערוך | או"ח תעב:ט

שיעור הכוס, רביעית לאחר שימזגנו (אם רוצה למזגו), וישתה כולו או רובו. ואם יש בו הרבה רביעיות,שותין ממנו כל כך בני אדם כמנין רביעיות שבו. ויש אומרים שצריך לשתות רוב הכוס, אפילו מחזיק כמה רביעיות.

The **Mishna Berura** rules that it is permissible to drink only the majority of a *revi'it* (i.e., a cheek-full). However, *lechatchila* (ideally) one should drink the entire cup or at least the majority of the cup. Therefore, he suggests that one should not use cups that are much larger than a *revi'it*. That way, one can still drink the entire cup or the majority and fulfill one's obligation according to all opinions.

א | Mishna Berura 472:33

The majority of the cup – Although in general it is sufficient to have a majority of a *revi'it*, even from a large cup; here regarding the four cups it is more stringent, as the majority of the cup is required, and if he has not [drunk that amount] he hasn't fulfilled his obligation. However, practically the halacha is in accordance with the first opinion. Nevertheless, if one does not plan on drinking a lot, one shouldn't take a large cup, but a smaller cup that holds a *revi'it* in order to take this opinion into consideration.

10. משנה ברורה | תעב:לג

רוב הכוס אפי' וכו' – אף שבעלמא די ברוב רביעית אפילו מכוס גדול הכא לענין כוסות חמיר טפי דבעינן דוקא רוב כוס ואם לאו לא יצא. ולדינא קיי"ל כדעה הראשונה. ומ"מ אם אין בדעתו לשתות הרבה לא יקח כוס גדול רק כוס שמחזיק רביעית כדי לחוש לדעה זו.

Regarding the manner of drinking, the **Rema** writes that "one needs to drink without a large break in between."

The **Mishna Berura** writes that *lechatchila* one should drink the entire amount at once, but if that is difficult, one should be stringent to at least drink it within the amount of time necessary to drink a *revi'it* (which is two gulps one after the other – **Shaar Hatziyun** 11). *Bedieved* (after the fact), if he drank the amount within the time of *achilat pras* (the amount of time necessary to eat half a loaf of bread – four minutes according to the stringent opinions), he has fulfilled his obligation.

א | Mishna Berura 472:34

Without a large break – Meaning that one must not delay the amount of time of *achilat pras* while drinking the majority of the cup. If one did delay for more than this amount of time, the initial drinking is not combined with the latter drinking, and one hasn't fulfilled one's obligation even *post facto*, and one needs to repeat drinking even regarding the latter cups [the third and fourth]. And there is no problem of adding additional cups, since according to all, one hasn't fulfilled one's obligation.

Lechatchila one should be careful when drinking the majority of the cup **not to delay more than the time it takes to drink the majority of a *revi'it*.** This is in order to take into consideration the first opinion brought in *siman* 612. Nevertheless, *post facto* if one did delay during the last two cups, one does not repeat drinking… But for the first two cups one must return and drink. *Lechatchila* (ideally) one should drink the majority of a *revi'it* at one time.

11. משנה ברורה | תעב:לד

שלא בהפסק גדול – דהיינו שלא ישהה בשתיית רוב הכוס יותר מכדי אכילת פרס ואם שהה יותר משיעור זה אין מצטרף תחלת השתיה לסופה ואפילו בדיעבד לא יצא וצריך לחזור ולשתות אפילו בכוסות אחרונות [דאין כאן משום מוסיף על הכוסות כיון דלכו"ע לא יצא].

ולכתחלה יש ליזהר **שלא לשהות בשתיית** רוב הכוס יותר מכדי שתיית רביעית לחוש לדעה ראשונה המבואר בסימן תרי"ב ע"ש ומ"מ בדיעבד אם שהה בשתי כוסות אחרונות לא יחזור וישתה... ובשתי כוסות ראשונות יחזור וישתה. **ולכתחלה נכון לשתות רוב הרביעית בבת אחת.**

The Size of the Cup

Every *kos shel beracha* must big enough to contain at least a *revi'it* of wine, but the amount of a *revi'it* is subject to dispute among the *poskim*. **Rav Chaim Na'eh** holds that the measurement is 86 cc (the *gematria* of the word *kos* in Hebrew, כוס, is 86), which is about 3 ounces, while the **Noda B'Yehuda** and the **Chazon Ish** hold that it is 150 cc (the *gematria* of the words *kos hagun* in Hebrew), approximately 5 ounces.

The *Mishna Berura* (in the quote below from the ***Bi'ur Halacha***) rules that the practical halacha is that with regard to biblical mitzvot, one should adopt the stringent opinion, but for rabbinic mitzvot one may be lenient and rely on the smaller measurement. Since the four cups are rabbinic in nature, one may use the measurement of 86 cc as the size of a *revi'it*.[3]

| א | Bi'ur Halacha, Siman 271 | 12. ביאור הלכה | סימן רעא |

In practice it seems that regarding a Torah obligation such as consuming a *kezayit* of matza on the night of Pesach, one certainly needs to be stringent in accordance with them [the stringent opinions]. Similarly, regarding the nighttime *Kiddush*, whose basis is from the Torah, *lechatchila* one should also take the opinion of the *Tzelach* [i.e., R. Landau, who is also the author of the *Noda B'Yehuda*] into consideration. Similarly, the *Chatam Sofer* is stringent like him concerning the measurement of a *revi'it*.[4]

[However, regarding the daytime *Kiddush* and other instances of a *kos shel beracha*, one may rely on the common custom in accordance with what is explained in the *Magen Avraham* and *Pri Megadim* and other *Acharonim*]. Nevertheless, it seems that *lechatchila*, the cup should be capable of containing the volume of two eggs with their shell.

ולמעשה נראה דלענין דאורייתא כגון כזית מצה בליל פסח בודאי יש להחמיר כדבריהם וכן לענין קידוש של לילה דעיקרו הוא דאורייתא ג"כ נכון לחוש לכתחילה לדברי הצל"ח הנ"ל וכן בחתם סופר מחמיר ג"כ לענין רביעית כדבריו. [ומיהו לענין קידוש שחרית ולשאר כוס של ברכה יש לסמוך על מנהג העולם שנוהגין כמבואר במ"א ופמ"ג וש"א] ועכ"פ יראה לכתחלה שיחזיק הכוס כשני ביצים עם הקליפה וכנ"ל.

---

3. Rav Yosef Zvi Rimon (*Haggada Kinor David*, p. 36) notes that some have a custom to use a cup that contains 150 cc for the first cup of *Kiddush*, which is based on a Torah obligation (even though the obligation to say it over wine is only rabbinic in nature, and even though on *Yom Tov* most *poskim* hold the obligation is only rabbinic – see *Mishna Berura* 271:2). This custom is especially pertinent when Pesach falls out on Friday night, and the *Kiddush* is in fact a Torah obligation, as pointed out as well by Rav Shimon Eider (The Laws of Pesach p. 229). Rav Eider there also mentions that according to Rav Moshe Feinstein (in *Sefer Kol Dodi*, written by his son Rav Dovid Feinstein), the larger amount to be used specifically on Friday night equals 4. 42 fluid ounces. However, Rav Rimon notes that even this stringency need be practiced only by the one reciting *Kiddush*. [Addition of the English editors]

4. These sources here are referring to the dispute of whether we must double the halachic measurements of eggs nowadays due to the possibility that our eggs are half the size of what they once were (see footnote 9 below and the sources quoted there). The connection between the size of eggs and the size of a *revi'it* discussed here is that a *revi'it* (one fourth of a *log*) was equal to the size of 1. 5 eggs (as the *log* measurement was equal to six eggs). [Addition of the English editors]

RECLINING

One of the mitzvot of the Seder night is to recline on one's left side while eating and drinking, as stated by the Mishna (*Pesachim* 99b): "Even a poor person in Israel may not eat unless he reclines." The Gemara (*Pesachim* 108a) clarifies that the mitzva applies specifically while drinking the four cups and eating the matza and *Afikoman*. The reason for reclining is given by the **Rambam** as follows:

 Rambam, Commentary on the Mishna, Pesachim 10:1

13. פירוש המשנה לרמב"ם | פסחים י:א

They obligated one to eat while reclining in the manner of kings and distinguished individuals so that it should be in a manner of freedom.

וחייבוהו לאכול כשהוא מיסב כדרך שאוכלין המלכים והגדולים. כדי שיהיה דרך חרות.

 Rambam, Hilchot Chametz Umatza 7:6–7

14. רמב"ם | הל' חמץ ומצה ז:ו–ז

6. In every generation, a person is obligated to depict himself as if he himself came out of slavery in Egypt right now...

7. Therefore, when one eats on this night, he must eat and drink while reclining in a manner of freedom.

ו. בכל דור ודור חייב אדם להראות את עצמו כאילו הוא בעצמו יצא עתה משעבוד מצרים...

ז. לפיכך כשסועד אדם בלילה הזה צריך לאכול ולשתות והוא מיסב דרך חירות.

The basis for this rabbinic enactment of *haseiba* was the fact that reclining luxuriously in this manner was a common practice in Talmudic times. However, it seems that even in the times of the *Rishonim*, it was already not as widely practiced. The question that arises, therefore, is whether the mitzva of *haseiba* should still apply even if the basis for it is no longer relevant. The **Ra'avyah** suggests that since reclining is no longer considered a manner of freedom even for kings, the obligation of *haseiba* no longer applies.

 Ra'avyah, Volume 2, Pesachim 525

15. ראבי"ה | חלק ב, פסחים תקכה

In our times, where it is not common in our countries for free people to recline, one should sit normally.

ובזמן הזה שאין רגילות בארצינו להסב שאין רגילות בני חורין להסב ישב כדרכו.

The **Shulchan Aruch** rules that one must recline even today and describes the proper way to do so. If one does not do so, he rules that one has not fulfilled one's obligation, and must fulfill the mitzva in question again. For Sephardim, this ruling applies to all four cups of wine, while for Ashkenazim this is true for the first two cups only.

א Shulchan Aruch, Orach Chaim 472:3, 7

3. Shulchan Aruch: When one reclines, one should not lean backwards nor forwards, not to one's right; rather to one's left.

Rema: And there is no distinction between a left-handed person and another [i.e., right-handed person].

7. Shulchan Aruch: Regarding one who is obligated to recline, if he ate or drank without reclining he has not fulfilled his obligation and needs to repeat eating and drinking while reclining.

Rema: Some say that in today's times, where it is not the norm to recline, we may rely on the Ra'avyah in that after the fact, one has fulfilled one's obligation without reclining. **And it seems to me that if one didn't drink the third or fourth cup while reclining, he shouldn't drink again while reclining, as there is a concern that it seems that one is adding to the cups.** But for the first two cups, one drinks them again without a *beracha*, and similarly regarding eating matza. *Lechatchila*, one should recline for the entire meal.

16. שולחן ערוך | או"ח תעב:ג, ז

ג. כשהוא מיסב לא יטה על גבו ולא על פניו ולא על ימינו, אלא על שמאלו.

(ואין חילוק בין אטר לאחר)

ז. כל מי שצריך הסיבה, אם אכל או שתה בלא הסיבה לא יצא, וצריך לחזור לאכול ולשתות בהסיבה.

הגה: ויש אומרים דבזמן הזה, דאין דרך להסב, כדאי הוא ראבי"ה לסמוך עליו שבדיעבד יצא בלא הסיבה. ונראה לי אם אם לא שתה כוס שלישי או רביעי בהסיבה, אין לחזור ולשתות בהסיבה דיש בו חשש שנראה כמוסיף על הכוסות; אבל בשני כוסות ראשונות, יחזור וישתה בלא ברכה, וכן באכילת מצה. ולכתחלה יסב כל הסעודה.

Regarding women's obligation to recline, the **Shulchan Aruch** and **Rema** rules as follows:

א Shulchan Aruch, Orach Chaim 472:4

A woman does not need to recline unless she is prominent.

Rema: All of our women are considered prominent, but they do not have the custom to recline, as they rely on the words of the Ra'avyah who writes that in contemporary times one does not recline.

17. שולחן ערוך | או"ח תעב:ד

אשה אינה צריכה הסיבה אלא א"כ היא חשובה.

הגה: וכל הנשים שלנו מיקרי חשובות, אך לא נהגו להסב כי סמכו על דברי ראבי"ה דכתב דבזמן הזה אין להסב.

According to the *Shulchan Aruch* (based on the Gemara), women are exempt from reclining unless they are considered prominent, as apparently in earlier times most women never reclined, and it was never considered an expression of freedom for them to do so. By contrast, the Rema writes that even though all women have the status of prominent ones in former times, the custom is that no women recline based on the opinion of the Ra'avyah.[5] However, they are permitted to recline if they so desire, and it is considered praiseworthy for them to do so. Indeed, in practice many Ashkenazi women do customarily recline. With regard to the practice of Sephardic women, the **Ben Ish Chai** writes that the custom is to recline (which is also the opinion of **Rav Ovadia Yosef** in *Chazon Ovadia* 14).

---

5.   The *Aruch HaShulchan* (472:6) questions why the Rema states that women specifically rely on the opinion of the Ra'avyah. If his opinion is accepted, then why don't men also rely on it? Rav Shlomo Zalman Auerbach (*Halichot Shlomo*, Pesach chapter 9) gives the following answer: According to the letter of the law, there is good reason to say that the halacha of reclining should no longer apply, as no one is accustomed to reclining nowadays and it is not considered an expression of freedom anymore. Nevertheless, we still recline because our ancestors did so, in commemoration of their custom. But this is the case with regard to men only, who used to recline, and therefore continue the custom of previous generations. Most women though never had the practice of reclining (as noted in the text). Since they never did so initially, they are exempt now as well from continuing the custom.

| א | Ben Ish Chai, Shana Rishona, Parshat Tzav, Se'if 28 |

18. בן איש חי | שנה ראשונה, פרשת צו סעיף כח

...Also all the four *kezayit* portions of matza need to be eaten while reclining, both for men and women, adults and children...

...וגם אכילת כל ארבע כזייתות של מצה יהיו בהסיבה, בין אנשים ובין הנשים בין הגדולים בין הקטנים...

RABBI YOSEF CHAIM – THE BEN ISH CHAI (1835–1909)

Rav Yosef Chaim of Baghdad, often known by the name of his work the *Ben Ish Chai*, was a leading Sephardic Torah scholar, Kabbalist, and authority on Jewish law. Born to a family of distinguished rabbis, Yosef Chaim became well-versed in Torah and Kabbala at a young age. For years, he would seclude himself in a special room used for study and strive to attain spiritual perfection. At twenty-five, he was appointed as the leading rabbi of Baghdad upon his father's death.

Rav Yosef Chaim gave regular daily and weekly lectures to the Jews of Baghdad that fused together the weekly parsha, Kabbala, and halacha, and was venerated by his congregants, who followed his every ruling scrupulously. These lectures were ultimately transformed into his famous work *Ben Ish Chai*, which is still studied by thousands today. Rav Yosef Chaim was known as a pious and saintly individual, and his halachic rulings also often combine mystical and Kabbalistic elements. He is still considered one of the most influential *poskim* with regard to practical halacha for many Sephardic Jews today, though his works are cited as well in Ashkenazi halachic literature. In addition to the *Ben Ish Chai*, he also authored numerous other works on all areas of Torah, including *Ben Yehoyada* on the Aggadic sections of the Talmud, poetry and works on *Tefilla*, responsa published under the names *Torah Lishma* and *Rav Pealim*, and *Mekabtziel*, an elaboration on some of the topics discussed in the *Ben Ish Chai*.

URCHATZ

Following *Kiddush*, we wash our hands before eating the *karpas*, based on the halacha of *davar shetibulo bemashkeh,* washing hands for any vegetable dipped in a liquid, which is cited elsewhere in the *Shulchan Aruch* as applying all year round. However, since *Rishonim* dispute whether there is in fact an obligation to do so today (and many today rely on the lenient opinions not to do so at all), we wash our hands without a *beracha*.

א **Shulchan Aruch, Orach Chaim 473:6**   **19. שולחן ערוך | או"ח תעג:ו**

One washes one's hands for the sake of the first dipped vege-   נוטל ידיו לצורך טיבול ראשון ולא יברך על
table, but one does not recite a *beracha* on the washing…   הנטילה...

א **Mishna Berura 158:20**   **20. משנה ברורה | קנח:כ**

Since there are a few *Rishonim* who hold that the Sages did not   כי יש מקצת הראשונים דסברי שלא הצריכו
require washing hands for vegetables that have been dipped in   חכמים נט"י לדבר שטיבולו במשקה אלא
liquid except in their days, where they were scrupulous about   בימיהם שהיו אוכלים בטהרה משא"כ עכשיו
eating in a state of purity, as opposed to nowadays where we are   שכולנו טמאי מתים ולכך לא יברך ענט"י
all impure with impurity of a corpse [*tamei meit*]. Therefore   שספק ברכות להקל.
one should not recite a *beracha*, as uncertainties with regard
to *berachot* are resolved leniently [i.e., not reciting a *beracha*].

KARPAS

Once everyone has washed their hands, the Seder continues with the eating of the *Karpas* vegetable, as described by the **Mishna**.

 Masechet Pesachim 114a | **21. מסכת פסחים קיד.**

The attendants **brought** vegetables **before** the leader of the Seder prior to the meal, if there were no other vegetables on the table. **He dips the *chazeret*** into water or vinegar… **so that there be a conspicuous** distinction **for the children.**

הביאו לפניו מטבל בחזרת... כי היכי דליהוי היכירא לתינוקות.

How Much *Karpas* is Eaten?

According to the **Rambam**, one must eat a *kezayit* of *Karpas*, as eating an amount less than a *kezayit* is not considered significant in halacha. This is the ruling of the **Bach** (*siman* 473) and the **Gra** (*Ma'aseh Rav* 187) as well.

 Rambam, Hilchot Chametz Umatza 8:2 | **22. רמב"ם | הל' חמץ ומצה ח:ב**

One begins by reciting the *beracha* of *borei pri ha'adama* and then takes a vegetable and dips it in *charoset* and eats a *kezayit*; he as well as all the people sitting with him, each person must not eat less than a *kezayit*.

מתחיל ומברך בורא פרי האדמה ולוקח ירק ומטבל אותו בחרוסת ואוכל כזית הוא וכל המסובין עמו כל אחד ואחד אין אוכל פחות מכזית.

However, the **Rosh** and the **Rashba** hold that one need not eat a *kezayit*, since the purpose of *Karpas* is only to pique the children's interest, as stated in the Mishna above.

 Rosh, Pesachim 10:25 | **23. רא"ש | פסחים י:כה**

…Because when reciting the *beracha* of "*al achilat maror*" (on eating *maror*), one needs to eat a *kezayit*, as it is not defined as eating with less than a *kezayit*. However, concerning the vegetables [that one eats] earlier and upon which one recites *borei pri ha'adama* but does not mention eating, one does not need [to eat] a *kezayit*.

...משום דמברך על אכילת מרור צריך שיאכל כזית דאין אכילה בפחות מכזית אבל בירקות הראשונות שמברך עליהן בפה"א בעלמא ואין מזכירין עליהם אכילה אין צריך מהם כזית.

The **Shulchan Aruch** rules in accordance with the Rosh and adds that one should specifically eat less than a *kezayit* in order not to enter into any doubt regarding whether a concluding *beracha* (*beracha acharona*) is required, and this is the accepted custom.

| א | **Shulchan Aruch, Orach Chaim 473:6** | **24. שולחן ערוך | או"ח תעג:ו** |

...One takes less than a *kezayit* of *karpas* and dips it in vinegar, and recites the *beracha* of *borei pri ha'adama* and then eats. One does not recite the concluding *beracha*.

...ויקח מהכרפס פחות מכזית ומטבלו בחומץ ומברך בורא פרי האדמה ואוכל, ואינו מברך אחריו.

If one did eat a *kezayit*, one should nevertheless not recite a *beracha acharona* because the *beracha* on *Karpas* is supposed to cover the consumption of the *maror* as well, as explained by the **Mishna Berura**.

| א | **Mishna Berura 473:55–56** | **25. משנה ברורה | תעג:נה–נו** |

55. **And recites the *beracha* of *borei pri ha'adama*** – And one should have intention to exempt the *maror* that one will eat later with this *beracha*.

56. **One does not recite the concluding *beracha*** – Even if one ate a *kezayit*, since the first *beracha* covers the *maror* as well.

נה. ומברך בורא פה"א – ויכוין לפטור בברכה זו גם המרור שיאכל אח"כ [אחרונים].

נו. ואינו מברך אחריו – אפילו אם אכל כזית לפי שברכה ראשונה קאי גם על המרור.

YACHATZ

On the Seder night one is supposed to eat a broken piece of matza instead of a whole matza, which is the reason for performing *Yachatz*, the breaking of the matza, prior to *Maggid*. This is similar to a poor person who doesn't have the means to procure a full loaf of bread, and suffices with a piece instead, as indicated by the **Gemara** below.

ח	Masechet Pesachim 115b	.26 מסכת פסחים קטו:

Shmuel said that the phrase: **"The bread of affliction [*lechem oni*]"** (*Devarim* 16:3) means **bread over which one answers [*onim*] matters,** i.e., one recites the *Haggada* over matza. **That was also taught** in a *beraita*: *Lechem oni* is bread over which one answers many matters. **Alternatively,** in the verse, "*lechem oni*" is actually **written** without a vav, which means a poor person. **Just as** it is **the manner of a poor** person **to** eat **a piece** of bread, for lack of a whole loaf, **so too, here** he should use **a piece** of *matza*.

אמר שמואל: לחם עני (כתיב) – לחם שעונין עליו דברים. תניא נמי הכי לחם עני – לחם שעונין עליו דברים הרבה. דבר אחר: לחם עני – עני כתיב, מה עני שדרכו בפרוסה – אף כאן בפרוסה.

The **Shulchan Aruch** describes the exact procedure followed for breaking the matza.

א	Shulchan Aruch, Orach Chaim 473:6	.27 שולחן ערוך	או"ח תעג:ו

…He takes the middle matza and breaks it into two pieces. He gives one half to one of those sitting [at the table] to keep for the *afikoman*, and this is placed under a cover, while he places the other half between the two whole matzot…

...ויקח מצה האמצעית ויבצענה לשתים, ויתן חציה לאחד מהמסובין לשומרה לאפיקומן ונותנין אותה תחת המפה, וחציה השני ישים בין שתי השלימות...

The **Pri Megadim** adds that one must be careful to break the bread in the manner of a poor person.

א	Pri Megadim, Orach Chaim, Aishel Avraham 473:20	.28 פרי מגדים	או"ח, אשל אברהם תעג:כ

With his hand and not with a knife, the way a poor person does.

ביד ולא בסכין, כדרך שהעני עושה.

Some have the custom to then place the broken matzot on their shoulders as a remembrance of the Exodus, as described by the *Mishna Berura*.

א	Mishna Berura 473:59	.29 משנה ברורה	תעג:נט

There are those that place it [the matza] on their shoulders as a remembrance of the Exodus.

יש שנותנין אותה על כתפיהם זכר ליציאת מצרים.

MAGGID

The next section of the Seder, *Maggid*, contains one of the primary mitzvot of the evening, the mitzva of telling the story of the Exodus. However, it is evident from the *sugya* in *Masechet Berachot* below (also brought in the *Haggada*) that there is a mitzva to remember *yetziat mitzrayim* every night of the year as well. In that *sugya*, Tannaim dispute why the Torah added the word "*kol*" in the verse "*kol yemei chayecha*," "all the days of your life," when describing the mitzva to remember the Exodus from Egypt. The halacha follows the opinion of Ben Zoma who explains that the word "*kol*" teaches that the Exodus must be remembered at night as well.

Masechet Berachot 12b | ‫30. מסכת ברכות יב:‬

The Exodus from Egypt is mentioned at night, adjacent to the recitation of *Shema*. **Rabbi Elazar ben Azarya said: I am like seventy years old, and** although I have long held this opinion, **I was never privileged** to prove that there is a biblical obligation to fulfill the accepted custom and have **the Exodus from Egypt mentioned at night, until Ben Zoma interpreted it homiletically** and proved it obligatory.

מזכירין יציאת מצרים בלילות. אמר רבי אלעזר בן עזריה: הרי אני כבן שבעים שנה, ולא זכיתי שתאמר יציאת מצרים בלילות עד שדרשה בן זומא. שנאמר: "למען תזכר את יום צאתך מארץ מצרים כל ימי חייך." ימי חייך – הימים, כל ימי חייך – הלילות; וחכמים אומרים: ימי חייך – העולם הזה, כל – להביא לימות המשיח.

As it is stated: "That you may remember the day you went out of the land of Egypt all the days of your life" (*Devarim* 16:3).

The days of your life, refers to daytime alone; however, the addition of the word "all," as it is stated: **"All the days of your life,"** serves to include the nights as well.

And the Rabbis explain the word "all" differently and **say: The days of your life,** refers to the days in **this world, all** is added **to include the days of the Messiah.**

Based on this, one may ask what is so unique about the Seder night, as every other night there is also an obligation to recall the Exodus from Egypt.

The *Acharonim* discuss this question at length and offer a number of answers distinguishing the unique obligation of telling the story on the Seder night from the mitzva in effect the rest of the year.

Minchat Chinuch, Mitzva 21 | ‫31. מנחת חינוך | מצוה כא‬

Now it seems that the Rambam requires further analysis, for he counted the mitzva to tell [the story of the Exodus] on the night of the 15th [as a separate mitzva]. But why is this night greater than all other nights, for there is a mitzva to remember the Exodus from Egypt every day and night… see Responsa *Sha'agat Aryeh* (*Hilchot Yetziat Mitzrayim*) who clarifies at length that one does not fulfill one's obligation (every night) by mental thought alone.

והנה לכאורה צריך עיון על הרמב"ם, דמונה המצוה לספר בליל ט"ו מאי מעליותא דליל זה מכל הלילות הא מצוה להזכיר יציאת מצרים בכל יום ובכל לילה... עיין שו"ת שאגת אריה הלכות יציאת מצרים האריך לברר שאינו יוצא ידי חובה בהרהור ולומר דבכל יום די בהזכרת יציאת מצרים לחוד

And to say that in general it is sufficient to mention the Exodus without the story, as opposed to here one needs to tell the miracles and wonders that Hashem may He be blessed did for us [also does not seem correct]… as it's possible that even on the Seder night, one fulfills one's obligation by mentioning it as well. See the *Pri Chadash* (*siman* 473) who states that one fulfills one's obligation by mentioning the Exodus during *Kiddush*. And see the Ran who writes that "anyone who didn't mention these three things on Pesach hasn't fulfilled his obligation" is only referring to fulfilling the mitzva in the best way possible… but he has fulfilled his obligation according to the Torah. According to what we have written, **one can say that generally the mitzva is to mention it to oneself and not tell it to one's child, whereas here the mitzva is to tell one's child.** But if there is no other person with him, the mitzva to mention it to oneself is equivalent to that of other nights…

Rav Chaim Soloveitchik of Brisk offers another answer.

בלא סיפור וכאן צריך סיפור הנסים ונפלאות שעשה עמנו השי"ת... דאפשר דגם בליל פסח יוצא בהזכרה לחוד.

ועיין פרי חדש סי' תע"ג דבהזכרת יציאת מצרים בקידוש יצא, ועיין ר"ן שכתב דכל שלא אמר ג' דברים אלו בפסח לא יצא י"ח היינו מן המובחר כראוי... אבל יצא י"ח מן התורה, ולפי מה שכתבנו אפשר לומר דתמיד המצוה להזכיר **בפני עצמו ולא להגיד לבנו וכאן המצוה לספר לבנו,** אבל אם אין עמו אחר, המצוה להזכיר בעצמו שוה לשאר הלילות...

.32 חידושי הגר"ח | פסחים קטז.

Chidushei HaGrach, Pesachim 116a

Regarding the mitzva of "and you shall tell your son":

Every night there is a mitzva of remembering the Exodus from Egypt, and if so what is added on the Seder night within the obligation to tell the story of the Exodus from Egypt that is beyond the remembering that we do all year round? **It seems that there are three differences between the mitzva of remembering [*zechira*] the Exodus from Egypt and the mitzva of telling [*sippur*] the story of the Exodus from Egypt.**

1. In order to fulfill the mitzva of *zechira*, one only needs to remind oneself about the Exodus, while the mitzva of *sippur yetziat mitzrayim* is to tell the story to someone else by way of question and answer, as it is written: "When your son will ask… and you shall say to him… and you shall tell your son, etc." In the *Haggada* the son asks *mah nishtana* (what is different on this night) and the father answers that we were slaves in Egypt. And the halacha is that even if one is by oneself, one must ask oneself [questions] and answer with *avadim hayinu* similar to [the manner in which would] tell the story to another person.

2. In telling the story, one needs to relate the entire development, and begin with the degradation and end with the praise [see *Pesachim* 115a]. However, to fulfill the mitzva of *zechira*, one only needs to mention the Exodus from Egypt.

במצות והגדת לבנך:

הנה בכל לילה יש מצוה של זכירת יציאת מצרים, וא"כ מה נתוסף בליל פסח במצות סיפור יציאת מצרים שאין בזכירה של כל השנה? ונראה לומר, שיש ג' חילוקים בין המצוה של זכירת יציאת מצרים להמצוה של סיפור יציאת מצרים:

א. לקיים מצות זכירה אין צריך אלא להזכיר לעצמו יצי"מ, אבל בסיפור יציאת מצרים המצוה היא לספר לאחר דרך שאלה ותשובה כדכתיב "והיה כי ישאלך בנך וגו' ואמרת אליו" וכדכתיב "והגדת לבנך וגו'." ובהגדה הבן שואל מה נשתנה והאב משיב עבדים היינו, וההלכה היא שאפילו אם אחד לבדו צריך לשאול לעצמו ולומר עבדים היינו כדרך סיפור לאחר.

ב. בסיפור צריך לספר כל ההשתלשלות, וצריך להתחיל בגנות ולסיים בשבח, ולקיים מצות זכירה סגי בזכירת יציאת מצרים לחוד.

2. In telling the story, one needs to relate the entire development, and begin with the degradation and end with the praise [see *Pesachim* 115a]. However, to fulfill the mitzva of *zechira*, one only needs to mention the Exodus from Egypt.

3. The mitzva (on Seder night) is to explain the reasons for the mitzvot of that night, as is brought in the Mishna (*Pesachim* 116a): Rabban Gamliel would say that anyone who didn't say these three things on Pesach did not fulfill his obligation and they are Pesach, matza and *maror*. Pesach due to what, etc., matza due to, etc., marror due to, etc."[6]

ב. בסיפור צריך לספר כל ההשתלשלות, וצריך להתחיל בגנות ולסיים בשבח, ולקיים מצות זכירה סגי בזכירת יציאת מצרים לחוד.

ג. מצוה לספר טעמי המצוות של אותו הלילה, כמ"ש במשנה (פסחים קטז ע"א) רבן גמליאל היה אומר כל שלא אמר שלשה דברים אלו בפסח לא יצא ידי חובתו, ואלו הן פסח מצה ומרור, פסח על שום מה וכו' מצה על שום וכו' מרור על שום וכו'.

As mentioned in Rav Chaim's first answer, the ideal mitzva of *sippur yetziat mitzrayim* involves telling the story to one's children or others in a question and answer form. Does this require a person to tell the story himself, or is it sufficient for someone else at the table to do so for him?

Rav Shlomo Zalman Auerbach addresses this question concerning a married son with children visiting his parents (or in-laws) where someone else at the table (e.g., the grandfather) will tell the story. Rav Shlomo Zalman rules that it is sufficient that any one of the people at the table tells the story, and it need not be specifically a father to his children.

❖ Halichot Shlomo, Pesach 9:31 | 33. הליכות שלמה | פסח ט:לא

If many people are sitting together [at the Seder], there is no obligation on each one of them to tell the story of *yetziat mitzrayim* to his children himself; rather, it is sufficient if one of the participants tells everyone.

רבים המסובים יחד, אין חיוב על כל אחד מהם לספר סיפור יציאת מצרים לבניו בעצמו, אלא די בכך שאחד המסובים יספר לכולם.

It is clear from these sources that the children (if there are) must be the focal point of the Seder and the telling of the story, as this is the purpose of this night: Transmitting our heritage and the basis for our nation and faith to the next generation. For this reason, the **Rema** stresses in the source below that one must ensure that the children are involved in the Seder experience and understand the story being told on their own level.

א Shulchan Aruch, Orach Chaim 473:6 | 34. שולחן ערוך | או"ח תעג:ו

...He lifts the plate that has the matzot on it and says [from] "This is the bread of affliction" until *Ma Nishtana*.

הא ...ויגביה הקערה שיש בה המצות ויאמר: לחמא עניא, עד מה נשתנה.

---

6. In the continuation of the piece, Rav Chaim writes that these three ideas are actually explicitly mentioned in the Rambam (*Hilchot Chametz Umatza* chapter 7) in the context of *sippur yetziat mitzrayim*. In halacha 1, he discusses the special role that children play at the Seder, that one must tell the story to them even if they don't ask about it, he should teach them according to their level, etc. In halacha 4, he discusses the concept of beginning with the degradation and concluding with the praise. And in halacha 5, he writes that anyone who has not discussed the three items of *pesach*, *matza*, and *maror* has not fulfilled his obligation. The Rambam then concludes that all of these ideas he has mentioned previously are considered aspects of the *Haggada*. The implication of the Rambam is that all three of the elements discussed here by Rav Chaim are included as a part of the mitzva of the *Haggada*, thus differentiating it from the daily mitzva of *zechira*.

Rema: They should say it in a language that women and children can understand, or explain to them the topic at hand. And this is what the Ri of Londari did [that he recited] the entire *Haggada* in the vernacular so that the women and children would understand.

Then he should instruct that it [the Seder plate] be removed from the table and placed at the end of the table as if one has already eaten, so that the children see this and ask [about it].

הגה: ויאמרו בלשון שמבינים הנשים והקטנים, או יפרש להם הענין וכן עשה ר"י מלונדרי כל ההגדה בלשון לע"ז, כדי שיבינו הנשים והקטנים.

ואז יצוה להסירם מעל השלחן ולהניחם בסוף השלחן כאלו כבר אכלו, כדי שיראו התינוקות וישאלו.

RACHTZA

The **Gemara** in **Pesachim** states that even though one has already washed his hands before eating the *Karpas*, one must wash his hands again before the *beracha* of *hamotzee* because he experienced a lapse of concentration (*hesach hada'at*) in between while reciting the *Haggada* and *Hallel*.

Masechet Pesachim 115b   35. מסכת פסחים קטו:

...**Why do I** need **two washings of** the **hands? He has** already washed his hands once. **They say** in response: **Since he needs to recite** the *Haggada* and *Hallel* in between the two dippings, **perhaps he will divert his thoughts and** his hands **will touch** a ritually impure object.

...למה לי נטילת ידים תרי זימני? הא משא ליה ידיה חדא זימנא! אמרי: כיון דבעי למימר אגדתא והלילא – דילמא אסוחי אסחיה לדעתיה ונגע.

The *Rishonim* write though that if one guarded his hands carefully and ensured they didn't touch anything unclean, he does not have to wash again.

Shibolei Haleket, Seder Pesach 218   36. שבולי הלקט | סדר פסח ריח

Since the reason is dependent on a lapse of concentration, if it is clear to him that he guarded his hands well and didn't touch holy scripture or other things that render his hands impure, he doesn't need to wash his hands again, for his hands are still pure from the first washing.

וכיון שתלה הטעם בהסח הדעת אם ברור לו ששימר ידיו היטב ולא נגע בכתבי הקודש או בשאר דברים המטמאין את הידים אינו צריך לחזור וליטול ידיו שהרי ידיו טהורות מנטילה ראשונה.

Nevertheless, the **Beit Yosef** rules that one should not follow this, in order not to nullify the decree of the Sages.

Beit Yosef, Orach Chaim Siman 475   37. בית יוסף | או"ח סימן תעה

It seems to me that one shouldn't do this intentionally, in order not to nullify a decree of the Sages, who instituted to wash [one's hands] two times on the night of Pesach.

ונראה לי, דאין לכוין בכך, שלא לבטל תקנת חכמים שתקנו ליטול פעמיים בליל פסח.

The **Bi'ur Halacha** writes that if one purposefully had no lapse of concentration, one should still wash one's hands, but without a *beracha*. He adds that the best suggestion in this scenario is for him to touch something unclean (e.g., using the bathroom), after which he may wash them and recite a *beracha*.

א **Bi'ur Halacha, Siman 475**　　　　　　　　**38. ביאור הלכה | סימן תעה**

One definitely needs to wash one's hands again (similar to what is written earlier in *siman* 168:7), especially if he did not intend from the outset [that the washing should relate to his] eating. Nevertheless, one should not recite a *beracha* (as was explained there). The best option in this case is to render one's hands unclean before washing so that he will be able to recite a *beracha*.

בודאי צריך לחזור וליטול ידיו וכדלעיל בסימן קנ"ח ס"ז ובפרט כשלא כוון מתחלה לאכילה עכ"פ אין לו לברך, וכמבואר שם והנכון שבאופן זה יטמא ידיו קודם הנטילה כדי שיוכל לברך.

MOTZEE-MATZA

The consumption of matza is another one of the primary mitzvot of the Seder night and is mentioned explicitly in the Torah. But the **Gemara** in *Masechet Pesachim* cites a dispute whether the eating of matza nowadays without the *korban pesach* (Paschal offering) is a Torah or rabbinic obligation.

Masechet Pesachim 120a | 39. מסכת פסחים קכ.

Rava said: The mitzva of **matza nowadays,** even after the destruction of the Temple, applies by **Torah** law; **but** the mitzva to eat **bitter herbs** applies **by rabbinic** law. **And** in **what** way **is** the mitzva of **bitter herbs different from** matza? **As it is written,** with regard to the Paschal offering: "They shall eat it **with matzot and bitter herbs**" (*Bamidbar* 9:11). **When there is** an obligation to eat **the Paschal offering, there is** likewise a mitzva to eat **bitter herbs; and when there is no** obligation to eat **the Paschal offering, there is** also **no** mitzva to eat **bitter herbs.**

אמר רבא: מצה בזמן הזה דאורייתא ומרור דרבנן. – ומאי שנא מרור דכתיב על מצות ומרים בזמן דאיכא פסח – יש מרור, ובזמן דליכא פסח – ליכא מרור. מצה נמי הא כתיב על מצות ומרים! – מצה מיהדר הדר ביה קרא בערב תאכלו מצת. ורב אחא בר יעקב אמר: אחד זה ואחד זה דרבנן.

But if so, the same reasoning should apply to **matza as well,** as **it is written:** "**With matzot and bitter herbs.**" **The verse repeats** the obligation to eat **matza,** as it states: "In the first month, on the fourteenth day of the month **in the evening, you shall eat matzot**" (*Shemot* 12:18). This verse establishes a separate obligation to eat matza, unrelated to the Paschal offering. **And Rav Acha bar Ya'akov said:** Nowadays, **both this,** the mitzva to eat matza, **and that,** the mitzva to eat bitter herbs, apply **by rabbinic** law.

The **Rambam** rules that eating matza is a Torah obligation, which is the ruling accepted by the other *Rishonim*.

Rambam, Hilchot Chametz Umatza 6:1 | 40. רמב"ם | הל' חמץ ומצה ו:א

There is a Torah commandment to eat matza on the night of the fifteenth day [of *Nisan*], as it is written: "In the evening, you shall eat unleavened bread" (*Shemot* 12:18), everywhere and for all time. It did not render the eating dependent upon the Paschal offering. Rather, this is an independent mitzva and the mitzva is in effect the entire night. But on the rest of the festival eating matza is optional; if one wants, one eats matza, if one wants he eats rice… But on the night of the fifteenth alone there is an obligation, and when one eats a *kezayit* (olive-size piece), one has fulfilled one's obligation.

מצות עשה מן התורה לאכול מצה בליל חמשה עשר שנאמר "בערב תאכלו מצות", בכל מקום ובכל זמן, ולא תלה אכילה זו בקרבן הפסח אלא זו מצוה בפני עצמה ומצותה כל הלילה, אבל בשאר הרגל אכילת מצה רשות רצה אוכל מצה רצה אוכל אורז... אבל בליל חמשה עשר בלבד חובה ומשאכל כזית יצא ידי חובתו.

On every Yom Tov, like Shabbat, there is an obligation of *lechem mishneh,* reciting the *beracha* of *hamotzee* at each meal on two whole *challot.* The *Rishonim* dispute whether the broken matza used on the Seder night may be counted for *lechem mishneh* or not, in which case another matza would need to be added.

🔊 Rashi, Pesachim 116a

So too here with the broken – [It is used] to recite the blessing *al achilat matza*, and two whole matzot are used for the *beracha* of *hamotzee*, for [the Seder night] is no worse than any other Yom Tov where one needs to recite the blessing [lit. cut] over two whole loaves. One recites the blessing over one of the whole matzot.

41. רש"י | פסחים קטז.

אף כאן בפרוסה – לברך על אכילת מצה ושתי שלימות מייתי, משום ברכת המוציא, דלא גרע משאר ימים טובים שצריך לבצוע על שתי ככרות שלימות, ובוצע מאחת מהשלימות.

According to **Rashi**, we require two whole matzot for the standard *beracha* of *hamotzee*, plus the broken matza for the additional *beracha* of *al achilat matza*. But the **Rambam** argues, stating the following:

🔊 Rambam, Hilchot Chametz Umatza 8:6

After that, he recites *al netilat yadayim* and washes his hand a second time, for he had a lapse of concentration while reading the *Haggada*. He takes two matzot, breaks one of them and places the broken part together with the whole matza and recites the blessing of *hamotzee lechem min ha'aretz* [the blessing on bread].

42. רמב"ם | הל' חמץ ומצה ח:ו

אחר כך מברך על נטילת ידים ונוטל ידיו שניה שהרי הסיח דעתו בשעת קריאת ההגדה, ולוקח שני רקיקין חולק אחד מהן ומניח פרוס לתוך שלם ומברך המוציא לחם מן הארץ.

The halacha is in accordance with the opinion of Rashi that we take three matzot and give a portion of the whole matza as well as of the broken matza to each person. But how much must one eat from each matza? The **Rosh** cited below offers his opinion:

🔊 Rosh, Pesachim 10:30

Therefore, the people are accustomed to taking three matzot… out of those three matzot, one breaks the middle one into two and keeps one half for the *Afikoman*, and leaves the other half between the whole ones. On the first [matza] one recites the *beracha* of *hamotzee*, and on the piece one recites the *beracha* of *al achilat matza*. **One eats both of them together, a *kezayit* from each one.** And one uses the third one for the sandwich of Hillel, for since they instituted three [matzot], we use each one for a mitzva. One who wants to properly fulfill both obligations should recite [the *berachot* of] *hamotzee* and *al achilat matza* and then cut up both the whole matza and the broken matza.

43. רא"ש | פסחים י:ל

הלכך נהגו העם לעשות שלש מצות... ומאותן שלש מצות יבצע השניה לשנים וישמור החציה לאפיקומן ויניח חציה בין שתי השלימות ועל הראשונה יברך המוציא ועל הפרוסה יברך על אכילת מצה **ואוכלן ביחד מכל אחת כזית** ומן השלישית יעשה כריכה כהלל דכיון דתיקון שלש מכל חדא נעביד בה מצוה חדא והרוצה לצאת ידי חובת שניהם יברך המוציא ועל אכילת מצה ויבצע מן השלימה ומן הפרוסה כאחד.

According to the Rosh, one must eat a *kezayit* of matza from each matza. The **Bach** wonders though why one must eat two separate *kezayit* portions. Why is an additional *kezayit* for *hamotzee* necessary in addition to the *kezayit* used for the mitzva of matza?

🇦 Bach, Orach Chaim Siman 475

Regarding what he wrote that one needs to eat a *kezayit* from each one, that is due to the fact that there is no definition of eating for less than a *kezayit* (*Pesachim* 32b; *Yerushalmi, Yoma* 2:1). However, this is astounding: One can understand [that one needs to eat a *kezayit*] from the piece of matza upon which one recites the *beracha al achilat matza*, it is logical that one needs [to eat] a *kezayit*. But regarding the whole matza upon which one recites the *beracha* of *hamotzee*, what is different from [the halacha of] other bread, upon which one recites *hamotzee* even though one doesn't eat a *kezayit*?

44. ב"ח | או"ח סימן תעה

ומה שכתב שיאכל כזית מכל אחד. היינו לפי שאין אכילה פחותה מכזית (פסחים לב:, ירושלמי יומא פ"ב ה"א) מיהו תימה בשלמא מן הפרוסה שמברך עליה על אכילת מצה שפיר דבעי כזית אבל מן השלמה שמברך עליה המוציא מאי שנא משאר פת שמברך עליו המוציא אף על פי שאינו אוכל כזית.

The **Shulchan Aruch** rules in accordance with the opinion of the Rosh and the **Mishna Berura** resolves all the questions of the *Bach*.

🇦 Shulchan Aruch, Orach Chaim 475:1

And he should eat a *kezayit* from each one simultaneously. If he is unable to eat two *kezayit* portions simultaneously, he should eat [the *kezayit*] of the *hamotzee* first and then [the *kezayit*] of *al achilat matza*.

45. שולחן ערוך | או"ח תעה:א

ויאכלם בהסיבה ביחד כזית מכל אחד, ואם אינו יכול לאכול כשני זיתים ביחד, יאכל של המוציא תחלה ואחר כך של אכילת מצה.

🇦 Mishna Berura 475:9

From the broken matza one definitely needs to eat a *kezayit*, for one recites the *beracha* of *al achilat matza* over this, and there is no definition of eating for less than a *kezayit*. However, regarding the broken matza used for *motzee*, we hold that we recite a *beracha* of *hamotzee* even over less than a *kezayit* (as discussed earlier in *siman* 210). However, since there are some *poskim* that hold that the *beracha* of *hamotzee* is recited over the broken matza and the *beracha* of *al achilat matza* is recited over the whole matza, therefore one needs [to eat] a *kezayit* from each.

46. משנה ברורה | תעה:ט

מן הפרוסה בודאי צריך כזית דהא מברכין על אכילת מצה ואין אכילה פחותה מכזית אבל פרוסת המוציא הלא קי"ל דהמוציא מברכין אפילו על פחות מכזית וכנ"ל בסימן ר"י אלא משום דיש פוסקין שסוברין דברכת המוציא קאי על הפרוסה וברכת על אכילת מצה קאי על השלמה לכך צריך מכל אחת כזית.

The **Mishna Berura** continues by stating that *bedieved* (after the fact), one fulfills one's obligation even if he ate only one *kezayit* from either of the matzot.

🇦 Mishna Berura 475:11

And then [the *kezayit*] of *al achilat matza* – Bedieved, if he ate one *kezayit* either from the whole matza or the broken matza, he has fulfilled his obligation.[7]

47. משנה ברורה | תעה:יא

ואח"כ של אכילת מצה – ובדיעבד אם אכל כזית אחד בין מהשלמה ובין מהפרוסה יצא.

---

7. It should be noted that some *poskim* limit the notion of eating two *kezayit* portions to the head of the household or one running the Seder alone, while everyone else may consume one *kezayit* alone. This is the opinion of Rabbi Akiva Eiger (on *Orach Chaim* 167), and is accepted as well by Rav Eliashiv (*Seder HaAruch*, p. 456).

We have already explained that ideally one should consume two *kezayit* portions at the Seder during *motzee-matza*. We now need to clarify the exact size of a *kezayit*, which is subject to a dispute among the *Rishonim*. The **Rambam** holds it is the size of a third of an egg (approximately 18 grams), while **Tosafot** hold it is the size of half of an egg (28 grams). The ***Shulchan Aruch*** rules in accordance with Tosafot:

א **Shulchan Aruch, Orach Chaim 486:1** | **48. שולחן ערוך | או"ח תפו:א**

[With regard to] the measurement of a *kezayit*, some say that it is half the size of an egg.[8]

שיעור כזית, יש אומרים דהוי כחצי ביצה.

It seems from the *Rishonim* that a *kezayit* should be measured by volume. However, a number of Sephardic *poskim* hold that the custom is to measure it by weight due to the difficulty of measuring by volume. According to this opinion, each *kezayit* measures approximately an entire standard machine matza.

א **Kaf Hachaim, Orach Chaim 168:45–46** | **49. כף החיים | או"ח קסח:מה-מו**

The accepted custom nowadays by G-d fearing people is to measure all the measurements i.e., a *kezayit* of matza on Pesach… by weight, and one should not deviate from this.

...וכן המנהג עכשיו פשוט אצל בעלי היראה לשער כל השיעורים דהיינו כזית מצה בפסח... כולם במשקל... ואין לשנות.

This is the ruling of most contemporary Sephardic *poskim* as well, such as **Rav Ovadia Yosef** and **Rav Mordechai Eliyahu** (see Responsa *Yechaveh Da'at* 1:16). By contrast, most Ashkenazi *poskim* measure a *kezayit* by volume, which measures approximately a third of a standard machine matza, as is brought by **Rav Eliezer Melamed** in the ***Peninei Halacha***.

♦ **Peninei Halacha, Hilchot Pesach 16:24** | **50. פניני הלכה | הל' פסח טז:כד**

It is clear according to the basic halacha that all halachic measurements are based on volume and not weight.

אולם מעיקר הדין ברור שכל השיעורים עוסקים בנפח ולא במשקל.

---

8. We should note that there is a very famous discussion of whether the size of eggs have decreased over the last few centuries. Some *poskim*, such as the *Noda B'Yehuda*, claim that they are now half the size of what they used to be, and therefore the measurements brought here must be doubled. According to the *Mishna Berura* (486:1), ideally this approach should be followed for mitzvot of Torah origin, such as eating matza at the Seder. Nevertheless, most *poskim* hold that if one is eating two *kezayit* portions in any case based on the previous few sources, it is unnecessary to double the measurements yet a second time, and doubling it once is sufficient. Although this is an extremely important issue, it is beyond the purview of this *shiur*. For more information, see the *Piskei Teshuvot* (486:2) and *Haggada Kinor David* by Rav Yosef Zvi Rimon (published by Mossad HaRav Kook in Hebrew and in English) in the section on *motzee-matza* at length. [Addition of the English editors]

Matza Shemura

The **Gemara** teaches that one is obligated to have *matza shemura,* "guarded matza," on Pesach.

Ⓗ Masechet Pesachim 40a | 51.מסכת פסחים מ.

Rava reconsidered and **then said:** It is not only permitted to soak the grains; it is actually **a mitzva to soak** them, **as it is stated: "And you shall guard the** *matzot*" (*Shemot* 12:17). The Gemara explains this statement: **If** it is **not** the case **that** grain **requires soaking, for what** purpose is **guarding** necessary? **If** you claim that this verse is referring to **guarding when kneading,** that cannot be the case, as **guarding** grain **while kneading is not** considered **guarding.** If one failed to protect the wheat from becoming leavened up to that point, it is of no use to be careful while kneading it. Consequently, this mitzva to guard the dough cannot be referring to the kneading stage.

As Rav Huna said: In the case of **dough** prepared **by gentiles,** if one knows that it has not become leavened, **a person** may **fill his stomach with them** on Passover night, **provided that he eats an olive-bulk of** *matza* **in the end,** to fulfill the obligation to eat *matza.* The Gemara infers from this statement: With regard to the *matza* that he eats **in the end, yes,** he fulfills his obligation with this *matza.* But with regard to the *matza* he ate **in the beginning, no,** he does not fulfill the mitzva with dough prepared by gentiles.

What is the reason that one cannot fulfill his obligation to eat *matza* with dough prepared by gentiles? It is **because** he **did not perform** his duty to **guard** this dough. **But one** can **perform** his duty to **guard it from** the time of **baking and onward. Rather, isn't it** correct to **conclude from** this *beraita* that the grain **must** be guarded **from the beginning…**

הדר אמר רבא: מצוה ללתות, שנאמר ושמרתם את המצות אי לא דבעי לתיתה – שימור למאי? אי שימור דלישה – שימור דלישה לאו שימור הוא, דאמר רב הונא: בצקות של נכרים אדם ממלא כריסו מהן, ובלבד שיאכל כזית מצה באחרונה. באחרונה – אין, בראשונה – לא. מאי טעמא – משום דלא עבד בהו שימור. ולעביד ליה שימור מאפיה ואילך! אלא לאו שמע מינה – שימור מעיקרא בעינן...

On a simple level, it seems from the Gemara that the dough must be guarded to ensure that it does not rise and become chametz. However, *Rishonim* dispute whether there is an additional element to this "guarding."

ㄱ Rambam, Hilchot Chametz Umatza 5:8 | 52.רמב"ם | הל' חמץ ומצה ה:ח

"And you shall guard the matzot" – Meaning that you must be careful with the matza and guard it from any possibility of becoming leaven.

"ושמרתם את המצות" – כלומר: הזהרו במצה ושמרו אותה מכל צד חמוץ.

ㄱ Rashi, Pesachim 38b | 53.רש"י | פסחים לח:

And you shall guard the matzot, make the guarding for the sake of matza – For all guarding that one does in order that it doesn't become *chametz,* have intention that it be for the sake of matza for the mitzva.

ושמרתם את המצות עביד לה שמירה לשם מצה – כל שימור שאתה משמרה שלא תחמיץ התכוון לשם מצה של מצוה.

According to **Rambam,** the primary requirement is to guard the matza from becoming chametz. According to **Rashi,** an active guarding is necessary with intention that the matza be suitable for the mitzva of eating matza. The **Mishna Berura** writes that *lechatchila*, we act in accordance with the opinion of Rashi.

א **Mishna Berura 453:21**	**54. משנה ברורה | תנג:כא**

This means that the matzot that we eat on the first two nights to fulfill the mitzva of "in the evening you shall eat matzot" require an additional element of guarding, and the fact that there is no concern that they might become chametz is not sufficient. Rather, we need an additional element of guarding for the sake of the mitzva of matza, as it is written, "and you shall guard the matzot," meaning that one needs to guard it for the sake of matza.

ר"ל המצות שאוכלין בשתי הלילות הראשונות לקיים מצות בערב תאכלו מצות הם צריכין שמירה יתירה ולא די לנו במה שאין לנו ריעותא של חשש חימוץ אלא שצריך שימור יתירה לשם מצות מצה דכתיב ושמרתם את המצות והיינו שצריך שישמור לשם מצה.

Commentaries further dispute in which stage the guarding must begin. There are three opinions regarding this, all of which are alluded to in the *Shulchan Aruch.*

א **Shulchan Aruch, Orach Chaim 453:4**	**55. שולחן ערוך | או"ח תנג:ד**

It is best to guard the wheat used for making matza for the mitzva that no water touch them from the time of harvesting, and at least [they should be guarded] from the time of grinding. In extenuating circumstances, it is permitted to take flour from the marketplace.

החטים שעושים בהם מצת מצוה טוב לשמרן שלא יפלו עליהם מים משעת קצירה, ולפחות משעת טחינה. ובשעת הדחק מותר ליקח קמח מן השוק.

According to the *Shulchan Aruch*, *lechatchila* one needs to guard the wheat from the time of harvesting, and if that is not possible, it should be guarded at least from the time of grinding. *Bedieved*, guarding from the time of kneading is also acceptable. Today, all matzot that are kosher for Pesach are *shemura* at least from the time of grinding, while those that are marketed as being "*shemura matza*" are guarded from the time of harvesting, as per the ideal of the *Shulchan Aruch*.

The *Shulchan Aruch*'s ruling here applies only to matza eaten on the first two nights (in the Diaspora), the "*matzat* mitzva," but during the rest of Pesach, there is no requirement to consume *shemura matza*. However, there are *Rishonim* that hold that one needs to eat *shemura matza* all seven days. The **Bi'ur Halacha** cites this opinion in the name of the **Rambam**, and this was also the custom of the **Vilna Gaon**.

א **Bi'ur Halacha 460:1**	**56. ביאור הלכה | תס:א**

See the Rambam, *Hilchot Chametz Umatza* 5:9, and it is clear from there that his opinion is that all matza that one eats on Pesach must be guarded.

ועיין ברמב"ם פ"ה מה' חמץ ומצה דין ט' ומוכח שם דדעתו דאכל מצה שאוכל בפסח צריך שימור.

The practical halacha is that on the first two nights, one must use *shemura matza* (ideally from the time of harvesting, but at least from the time of grinding). However, on the remaining days it is not necessary, though one who does so is praiseworthy.

◆ **Peninei Halacha, Hilchot Pesach p. 171**   **57. פניני הלכה | הל' פסח עמ' 171**

Some are careful to eat only *shemura matza* all of Pesach. There are two reasons for this: One is that some authorities hold that although there is no obligation to eat matza all of Pesach, nevertheless one who does eat has fulfilled a mitzva…

And the second reason is that some authorities hold that one of the reasons for eating *shemura matza* is due to the concern that it will leaven, and out of all our foods on Pesach, matza is the most likely to leaven. Therefore, if the wheat is not guarded from the time of harvesting, there is a concern that it may have become chametz.

יש מדקדקים לאכול בכל בכל הפסח מצות שמורות. ושני טעמים לכך: האחד, שיש סוברים שאמנם אין חובה לאכול מצות בכל הפסח, מכל מקום האוכל מקיים מצוה...

והטעם השני שיש סוברים שאחד מהטעמים לאכילת מצה שמורה הוא מפני חשש החימוץ, שכן מכל המאכלים שלנו בפסח המצה היא העלולה ביותר להחמיץ, ולכן אם לא ישמרו את החיטים משעת קצירה ישנו חשש שמא החמיצו.

Machine Matza

Ever since the beginning of the production of machine-made matza, it has been the subject of much controversy. Some *Acharonim* prohibited using it due to a concern of becoming chametz during the production as well as because perhaps machine matza is not considered to have been prepared for the sake of the mitzva (which might require a human element). Others, though, permitted it.

א **Responsa Avnei Nezer, Orach Chaim 537**   **58. שו"ת אבני נזר | או"ח תקלז**

I heard and my stomach has become ill for once again there are those who want to make machine matzot. Already the great and true *tzadikim*, his honor the Gerrer Rebbe *zt"l*, the holy Gaon of Tzanz *zt"l*, and the holy Gaon of Chechanov all prohibited using them definitively, for their impurity is on their side and underneath them shall remain the leprous mark, for it is chametz.[9]

שמעתי ותרגז בטני כי נתעורר מחדש לעשות מצות על מאשין. וכבר התעוררו הגאונים הצדיקים והאמתים ה"ה כבוד אדמו"ר זצ"ל מגור והגאון הקדוש זצללה"ה מסאנדז והגאון הקדוש זצללה"ה מטשעכנאווי לאסור אותם בהחלט יען כי טומאתם בשוליהם ותחתיהם תעמוד הבהרת כי חמץ המה.

---

9. This is a poetic manner (using the analogy of leprosy) of forcefully expressing the idea that the machine matzot would become chametz and therefore may not be used. [Addition of the English editors]

Mikra'ei Kodesh (by Rav Moshe Harari), Pesach Ch. 7, Footnote 79

59. מקראי קודש (הרב משה הררי) | פסח, פרק ז, הערה עט

The opinion of [some of] this generation's rabbis: Hagaon Rav Shlomo Zalman Auerbach told me that one may fulfill the obligation of the mitzva of matza at the Seder with machine matzot as well, and one may recite the *beracha* of *al achilat matza* on it. I asked him if there was a preference for hand-made matza or machine matza, and he answered me that if they supervise very well, then the hand-made matzot are preferable.

HaGaon Rav Ovadia Yosef writes that it is an ideal mitzva to try to take hand-made matza by G-d fearing people who are expert in halacha for the first night, in order to comply with all the opinions. Nevertheless, in extenuating circumstances one may fulfill his obligation on the first night with machine-made matzot as well, and one may even recite the *beracha* of *al achilat matza*. During the rest of the festival following the Seder night, even those who are careful to eat only *shemura matza* from the time of harvesting may eat machine-made matza…

דעת רבני דורנו: הגאון הרב שלמה זלמן אוירבך זצ"ל אמר לי שאפשר לצאת ידי חובה מצת מצוה בליל הסדר גם באכילת מצת מכונה, וכן אפשר לברך עליה את ברכת על אכילת מצה. ושאלתיו האם עדיפות מצות יד או מכונה, וענה לי שאם משגיחים "היטב היטב" אזי מצות יד עדיפות.

הגאון הרב עובדיה יוסף כתב שמצוה מן המובחר להשתדל לקחת למצת מצוה של הלילה הראשון מצה שמלאכתה נעשית בעבודת יד על ידי יראי שמים הבקיאים בהלכה, וזאת כדי לצאת ידי כל הדעות. ומכל מקום בשעת הדחק יוצאים ידי חובתו בלילה הראשון גם במצה הנעשית על ידי מכונה חשמלית, ואף רשאים לברך עליה את ברכת על אכילת מצה. ובשאר ימי החג לאחר ליל הסדר אף המקפידים לאכול רק מצה שמורה משעת הקצירה רשאים לאכול מצת מכונה...

In practice, one should ideally use hand-made matzot on the first two nights if possible, as this fulfills one's obligation according to all opinions. One who is unable to do so may rely on the *poskim* that hold that machine matzot are considered to be made *lishma,* for the sake of the mitzva (due to the presence of those supervising, who have this in mind). On the remaining days, where only the Rambam and those who follow his opinion recommend eating *shemura matza*, and in his opinion the definition of *shemura matza* is that it is properly guarded from chametz (and there is no need of intention for the sake of the mitzva), one can eat machine-made *shemura matza* even *lechatchila*, as today there is no concern of them becoming chametz when properly supervised.

Summary of Halachot of the Seder Night I

Kadesh

---

1. **The basis for the four cups**
   a. **Gemara** – Everyone is obligated in the mitzva of the four cups.
   b. **Rambam** – Drinking wine is an expression of freedom.
   c. **Rashi** – Four cups correspond to the four expressions of freedom in *Parshat Va'era*.

2. **The amount of wine one needs to drink for *Kiddush***
   a. **Tosafot** – A cheek-full.
   b. **Ramban** – The majority of the cup (and ideally the whole cup).
   c. *Shulchan Aruch* – Mentions both opinions.
   d. *Mishna Berura* – Ideally one should drink the majority of the cup, but *bedieved*, a cheek-full is sufficient.
   e. *Mishna Berura* – One should ideally drink it at one time.

3. **The size of the cup**
   a. Must contain a *revi'it* of wine.
   b. **Rav Chaim Naeh** – 86 cc.
   c. *Chazon Ish* – 150 cc.
   d. *Bi'ur Halacha* – For Torah obligations, the higher *shiur* should be used, while for rabbinic obligations (including the four cups), the lower *shiur* may be used.

4. **Reclining**
   a. **Rambam** – Reclining is an expression of freedom.
   b. **Ra'avyah** – Today it does not apply since people do not usually recline.
   c. *Shulchan Aruch* – Reclining must still be practiced today, though with regard to women, only prominent women must recline.
   d. **Rema** – Women follow the Ra'avyah and do not need to recline.
   e. *Ben Ish Chai* – Sephardic women should recline.

Urchatz

1. **Shulchan Aruch** – One washes hands but does not recite a *beracha*.

2. **Mishna Berura** – The reason is to fulfill the opinions that a food dipped in liquid requires *netilat yadayim*.

Karpas

1. **Mishna** – One dips the vegetable so that there should be a distinction for the children.

2. **Rambam** – One must eat a *kezayit* of *Karpas*.

3. **Rosh** – Less than a *kezayit* is enough.

4. **Shulchan Aruch** – One should specifically eat less than a *kezayit* to avoid doubts concerning the *beracha acharona*.

5. **Mishna Berura** – Even if one ate a *kezayit,* one does not recite a *beracha acharona*.

Yachatz

1. **Gemara/Shulchan Aruch** – One breaks the matza in two as a poor man does, keeping one to use later for *afikoman*.

Maggid

1. **Gemara Berachot** – Ben Zoma holds one must mention *yetziat mitzrayim* every night, and this is the halacha.

2. **How, then, is telling the story on Pesach night different from all other nights?**

   a. *Minchat Chinuch* – On Pesach night the mitzva is to tell another person.

   b. **Rav Chaim Soloveitchik** – There are other unique aspects to the mitzva on the Seder night.

      i. Questions and answers.

      ii. Must begin with the negative part of the story and conclude with the positive.

      iii. Must give the reason behind the mitzvot of the night.

   c. **Rema** – One must ensure that everyone at the table can understand the telling of the story.

Rachtza

1. **Gemara** – One must wash again in case his hands have become unclean during the interim.

2. *Beit Yosef* – Don't intentionally try to keep one's hands clean.

3. *Bi'ur Halacha* – Even if they are clean, one still washes but without a *beracha*.

Motzee-Matza

1. **Gemara** – It is a dispute whether the obligation is from the Torah or a rabbinic one.

2. **Rambam** – The halacha is that it is a Torah obligation.

3. **Rashi** – Two whole matzot are needed for *lechem mishneh* aside from the broken one. This position is accepted as halacha.

4. **Rambam** – The broken matza counts as one of the two for *lechem mishneh*.

5. **Rosh** – One must eat a *kezayit* from each matza.

6. *Mishna Berura* – One has fulfilled the obligation if one ate only one *kezayit*.

7. *Shulchan Aruch* – The halacha is in accordance with the opinions that a *kezayit* is half the size of an egg.

8. **Most *poskim*** – One measures the *kezayit* by volume.

9. *Kaf Hachaim* – Can measure the size of a *kezayit* by weight.

Matza Shemura

1. **Gemara** – There is an obligation to guard the matza.

2. **Rambam** – Guarding means to guard it from rising.

3. **Rashi** – Guarding it means guarding for the purpose of using for the mitzva of matza.

4. *Mishna Berura* – *Lechatchila* we are stringent for the opinion of Rashi.

5. *Shulchan Aruch* – Ideally it must be guarded from the time of harvesting, and at least from the time of grinding; today's *shemura matza* is from the time of harvesting.

6. **Rambam** – One should eat such matza all of Pesach.

7. ***Peninei Halacha*/other opinions** – There is no obligation to eat *shemura matza* during the rest of Pesach.

8. ***Avnei Nezer*** – One may not use machine matza on Pesach.

9. ***Mikraei Kodesh*** – Most *poskim* today allow using machine matza, though many recommend using hand matza for the Seder if possible.

FURTHER IYUN

The Fifth Cup in Halacha and Hashkafa

Rav Otniel Fendel (Participant, the Manhigut Toranit Program)

We are all familiar with the *minhag* to fill a fifth cup, commonly known as the cup of Eliyahu. What is the source for this *minhag*? Does it have any halachic significance, and how does it relate to the mitzva of drinking four cups of wine at the Seder?

The Mishna in *Masechet Pesachim*[1] concludes the order of the drinking of the four cups as follows:

מזגו לו כוס שלישי מברך על מזונו רביעי גומר עליו את הלל ואומר עליו ברכת השיר בין הכוסות הללו אם רוצה לשתות ישתה בין שלישי לרביעי לא ישתה.

They pour for him the third cup, and he recites over it Grace after Meals. [They pour] the fourth cup, he concludes *Hallel* over it and says *Birkat Hashir*. Between the [first two] cups, if one wishes to drink he may drink, but between the third and the fourth he may not drink.

The Mishna makes no mention of a fifth cup. However, the ensuing Gemara[2] quotes a *beraita* as follows:

The Rabbis taught: The fifth cup – one concludes *Hallel Hagadol* (the great *Hallel*)

over it; this is the opinion of Rabbi Tarfon. And others say, "G-d is my shepherd." The *beraita* brings both the opinion of Rabbi Tarfon and other *Tanna'im* who hold that there is a fifth cup; they only argue as to what is recited over it.

Although the *beraita* as we have quoted it is not the version that appears in the printed version of the text, it is the version quoted by the overwhelming majority of *Rishonim* (**Rif, Rambam, Ran, *Ba'al Hamaor*, Rosh**). How can we reconcile this *beraita* that states that there is a fifth cup with the Mishna mentioned above that only mentions four? Is this a *machloket Tanna'im*? If so, surely the Gemara should have pointed this out, as it often does: "*Mani matnitin, d'lo k'Rabbi Tarfon*," who is the author of the Mishna? It is surely not Rabbi Tarfon."[3]

Rashbam's Understanding of the Mishna and *Beraita*

The ***Yerushalmi***[4] explains that the reason one may not drink between the third and fourth cup is that one might become drunk, "for drinking during the meal (i.e., the preceding cups) doesn't

---

1. Mishna, *Pesachim* 10:7.
2. *Pesachim* 118a.
3. This question is raised by the *Milchamot Hashem*, Rosh, and Ran, among others.
4. *Yerushalmi, Pesachim* 10:6.

cause drunkenness, but after the meal does cause drunkenness."

The **Rashbam**,[5] commenting on the Mishna, brings the *Yerushalmi* and explains that the concern for drunkenness is that one won't be able to complete the *Hallel*. From the Mishna it is clear that there is no mention of a fifth cup, and based on the *Yerushalmi* and Rashbam, perhaps there is even a prohibition of reciting *Hallel Hagadol* over the fifth cup because it will turn out that one has drunk an intoxicating cup of wine (the fourth cup) before the conclusion of *Hallel*.

The **Rashbam** reconciles the *beraita* with the Mishna by stating that the correct version of the *beraita* is "the fourth cup" (and not "the fifth cup"). However, many *Rishonim* retain the version of the *beraita* citing a fifth cup, and the disparity between the Mishna and *beraita* therefore must be addressed.

Other Opinions of the *Rishonim*

The *Ba'al Hamaor*[6] and **Ra'avad** hold that the *beraita* indeed argues with the Mishna that stipulated four cups, but the *halacha* follows the Mishna, and not the *beraita*.[7] The *Ba'al Hamaor* does add though that if one wants to drink the fifth cup (even without reciting *Hallel Hagadol*), we cannot rebuke him, as it is permitted in principle.

The **Ramban**[8] understands that the *beraita* is not arguing with the Mishna. Rabbi Tarfon is merely adding that if one wants to drink a fifth cup, he needs to recite the *Hallel Hagadol* over

it. The Ramban explains that if one wants to drink wine after the four cups it is prohibited, as it looks like one is starting a second Seder (which would be prohibited from the Torah in the times of the *Beit Hamikdash*, for one cannot eat from two separate *korban pesachs*) unless he says *Hallel Hagadol* with it (which would show that this is actually an extension of the first Seder). The Ramban concludes, though, that the *minhag* of all of Israel is not to drink after concluding *Birkat HaShir*.

The **Ran**[9] suggests two ways to reconcile the Mishna and *beraita*. The first is similar to the Ramban: If one wants to drink more wine, one must recite *Hallel Hagadol* over it. His second answer is that it is actually a mitzva *min hamuvchar* – the best way to perform the mitzva – to drink the fifth cup and recite *Hallel Hagadol* over it. The Ran states that the opinion of the Rambam leans towards his second answer.

The **Rosh**[10] quotes **Rabbeinu Yonah** who prohibits drinking after the four cups of wine, as one has an obligation to learn the *halachot* of Pesach and tell the story of *yetziat mitzrayim* the entire night, and we are concerned that one might fall asleep due to the consumption of alcohol. Rabbeinu Yonah bases this on the Tosefta[11] that states: "One is obligated to occupy himself with the laws of Pesach the entire night."

In summary, some *Rishonim* hold that it is permitted (*Ba'al Hamaor*; *Hasagot HaRaavad* on the Rif) or even a mitzva (Ran and possibly Rambam) to drink the fifth cup, while others

---

5. Rashbam, *Masechet Pesachim* 118a s.v. *bein gimmel l'dalet lo yishteh.*
6. *Ba'al Hamaor* on the Rif, 26b s.v. *katav HaRif.*
7. The Ramban argues vehemently with the *Ba'al Hamaor* on this point.
8. *Milchamot Hashem* on the Rif.
9. Ran on the Rif, 26b s.v. *chamishi.*
10. Rosh, *Pesachim* 10:33.
11. Tosefta, *Pesachim* 10:8.

hold that it is prohibited to drink the fifth cup either according to the strict letter of the law (Rabbeinu Yonah and perhaps the Rashbam) or due to the accepted minhag (Ramban, Rosh).

What is the underlying argument between the *Rishonim* as to whether the fifth cup is forbidden, permitted, or recommended?

The Nature of the Mitzva of *Sippur Yetziat Mitzrayim*

Perhaps we can explain that this argument hinges on the very nature of the Torah obligation of *sippur yetziat mitzrayim*. One could posit that those *Rishonim* who prohibit drinking the fifth cup hold that the nature of the mitzva is not just to tell the story and praise Hashem, but also to focus on the *halachot* of Pesach, and in order to do this, one has to have lucidness and cannot be inebriated in any way (more than the four cups that the Sages instituted).

The **Griz**[12] explains that the Torah speaks to us in two different fashions: One is by way of story and narrative, and the other is by way of mitzvot, *chukim* and *halachot*. He parallels these two elements with the makeup of the *Haggada* and concludes explicitly that the mitzva of *sippur yetziat mitzrayim* on the Seder night includes both aspects: There is an obligation to tell the story of *yetziat mitzrayim* as well as an obligation to explain the practical mitzvot of the night.

On the other hand, the *Rishonim* who permit drinking the fifth cup understand that the focus of the mitzva of *sippur yetziat mitzrayim* is transmitting the story in any form, and if one wants to drink and tell it while inebriated, one still fulfills the obligation.[13]

The Scope of the Mitzva

Another understanding of the *machloket* is that it revolves around the scope of the mitzva. According to those who permit drinking, the mitzva is only until the latest possible time one can partake of the matza and maror.[14] However, according to Rabbeinu Yonah, the obligation exists the entire night until the morning, as mentioned in the Gemara and *Haggada* regarding Rabbi Akiva and the other *Tanna'im* in Bnei Brak.[15]

From Rabbeinu Yonah's words[16] it seems that he holds that both elements are true, namely that the nature of the mitzva of *sippur yetziat mitzrayim* includes learning the *halachot* of Pesach as well as the story, and the scope extends until the morning, and does not apply only during the meal. Accordingly, even if one has completed the meal, we are still concerned that a person should not become drunk, as the obligation of learning *Hilchot Pesach* is still incumbent upon him until dawn.

---

12. *Chidushei HaGriz Hachadashim*, siman 37.

13. See for example Rambam, *Sefer HaMitzvot* 157, where he stresses telling the story and singing and praising Hashem.

14. According to this approach, the deadline would be *chatzot*, in accordance with those opinions that give this as the deadline for consuming the *korban pesach* as well as the *afikoman*.

15. Rabbeinu Yonah himself in his *Seder Leil Pesach paskened* like Rabbi Elazar Ben Azaryah that one has to finish eating by *chatzot*. This seems to contradict how we have explained Rabbeinu Yonah here. Furthermore, Rabbeinu Yonah only mentioned the obligation of learning *Hilchot Pesach* and doesn't refer to continuing with *sippur yetziat mitzrayim* until dawn. One could argue that this is an independent obligation not connected to the mitzva of *sippur yetziat mitzrayim*. However, the *Tur* and Rosh quote him as including discussing *sippur yetziat mitzrayim* together with the obligation to study *Hilchot Pesach*; accordingly, it sounds like both are included within the mitzva of *sippur yetziat mitzrayim*. In the body of the article we have stated Rabbeinu Yonah's opinion based on how the *Tur* understood him. However, this matter requires further analysis.

16. *Tur* quoting Rabbeinu Yonah. See previous note.

When clarifying the opinion of the Rashbam we are left slightly in the dark. As mentioned previously, he states that the reason for not drinking between the cups is lest one becomes inebriated and is unable to recite *Hallel.* Arguably, after *Hallel* is recited on the fourth cup, he might not have a problem of adding a fifth cup. This is how the *Ba'al Hamaor* understood his opinion. On the other hand, the Rashbam earlier in his commentary brings another reason for not drinking in between the third and fourth cup[17] that it looks as if one is adding onto the cups instituted by the Sages. This reason might apply even after the end of the Seder. Alternatively, there might not be a problem of adding once the Seder has ended. Yet another possibility is that the Rashbam would actually agree with Rabbeinu Yonah as we have explained him above.

The Opinion of the Ran and Rambam Revisited

As mentioned, according to the Ran's second answer, it is actually a mitzva *min hamuvchar* to drink the fifth cup over *Hallel Hagadol.* The Ran states that the words of the Rambam lean toward this understanding as well. However, the actual words of the **Rambam** are somewhat ambiguous, as he states as follows:[18]

> And afterwards, he recites the *birkat hamazon* over a third cup and **drinks** it. And afterwards, he **pours** a fourth cup and finishes the *Hallel* over it. And he recites the *Birkat*

HaShir and that is: May all of your creatures praise you, etc. And he recites the blessing *Borei Pri Hagefen* and does not taste anything afterwards the entire night, except for water. And he should **pour a fifth cup** and say upon it the *Hallel Hagadol (Tehillim* 136)... **And this cup is not obligatory like the other four cups.**

The Ran understands that the word *limzog* (to pour) means to drink. The fact that the Rambam used this language regarding the other cups as well might support this as well. Furthermore, he states that this fifth cup isn't an obligation similar to the four cups, implying that it may be drunk, just that the level of obligation is different.[19]

What is the logic behind the opinion of the Ran (and possibly Rambam)? The opinions which forbid a fifth cup seem logical because the nature or timeframe (or both) of the mitzva of *sippur yetziat mitzrayim* do not allow for excessive drunkenness. However, the opinions of the Rambam and Ran seem puzzling: If the mitzva of *sippur* can co-exist with (and perhaps even be enhanced by) drunkenness, why, then, is the fifth cup only recommended and not obligatory like the other four?

The **Netziv**[20] explains the distinction of the Rambam and Ran between the obligatory four cups of wine and the fifth cup, which is only a mitzva *min hamuvchar,* in the following way. The first four cups parallel the four expressions of redemption. The fifth cup parallels the expression "*veyadatem et Hashem* – And you will know

---

17. Rashbam, *Pesachim* 108a, s.v. *bein shelishi.*

18. Rambam, *Hilchot Chametz Umatza* 8:10.

19. On the other hand, one could argue that the Rambam only mentioned pouring and did not state that one drinks or says a *beracha,* something that he stated regarding the other cups. This implies that here he only pours but does not actually drink it. In addition, the Rambam's formulation "and does not taste anything afterwards the entire night, except for water," which clearly refers to liquids, also implies that the fifth cup is not drunk. If it were drunk, the Rambam probably would have mentioned it before giving this general principle that nothing may be consumed after the cups.

20. *Meromei Hasadeh, Pesachim* 118a.

Hashem,"[21] which expresses a certain level of knowing Hashem through *Ruach Hakodesh* and prophecy which was not accessible to all. Hence, it was never instituted as an obligation. He states further that since today we no longer have prophecy until Eliyahu HaNavi will return, the *minhag* arose that no one drinks the fifth cup. This is the reason that we now refer to the fifth cup as the cup of Eliyahu.

A Second Explanation of the Rambam and Ran

Rav Eliashiv[22] explained that in relation to the *Afikoman* and the drinking of the four cups of wine, according to Rabbi Elazar Ben Azarya the four cups of wine are also only until midnight, for the telling of *yetziat mitzrayim* must be "at the time when matza and maror are placed in front of you." If so, the *chiyuv* of telling the story of *yetziat mitzrayim* extends specifically until midnight. However, if one started beforehand, one can continue as an extension of the original obligation. Accordingly, this could be another explanation for the distinction of the Rambam and Ran. According to the Rambam and Ran there is no independent obligation to tell the story the entire night, rather it is an extension of the original mitzva and has a special *geder* of mitzva *min hamuvchar,* and one who does so is praised. However, it is not an independent

obligation and hence, the Sages never instituted the fifth cup as an obligation, for this would imply a new and independent obligation. Furthermore, we now understand why Rabbi Tarfon stated that one must recite *Hallel Hagadol* over the fifth cup. This is not a new obligation, but an extension of *Hallel Hamitzri* and *Nishmat.* Drinking the fifth cup without reciting *Hallel Hagadol* would signify some independent obligation which doesn't exist.

This is in contrast to Rabbeinu Yonah and possibly the Rashbam who held that the obligation continues the entire night.

The Fifth Cup in Halacha

The *poskim* also have differing opinions regarding the fifth cup, which are based on many of the different principles and approaches outlined by the *Rishonim,* as we will see.

The **Shulchan Aruch**[23] does not mention a fifth cup at all, and the **Rema**[24] only mentions that someone who has a great need to drink may drink a fifth cup provided that he recites *Hallel Hagadol* on the cup. However, the **Chok Yaakov**[25] states one should fill (*limzog*) one extra cup, and this is called the cup of Eliyahu HaNavi.[26] This is also mentioned by the *Shulchan Aruch Harav.*[27]

The simple understanding of the *Chok Yaakov* is that we only pour the fifth cup,[28] not drink it, and other *Acharonim* do not mention drinking

---

21. *Shemot* 6:7.

22. *He'arot Rav Eliashiv, Masechet Pesachim* 120b.

23. *Shulchan Aruch* o.c. 480.

24. 481:1.

25. *Chok Yaakov* o.c. 480:6.

26. The *Chok Yaakov* also brings the *minhag* that in many places, people do not lock their rooms that they sleep in on the Seder night, so that if Eliyahu HaNavi comes, he will find the door open and we will run out to greet him. He noted that there is support for this custom from the *Talmud Yerushalmi.*

27. *Shulchan Aruch Harav* 480:45.

28. Although the Ran argued that when the Rambam used the word *limzog,* he meant to drink it; here it seems more difficult to say that this is the intention of the *Chok Yaakov:* The Rambam used that language for the other cups as well, and also compared

it either. At the very least though, we have a later source that records the custom of adopting the notion of the fifth cup in some manner.

The *Chok Yaakov* also adds a novelty that this cup connects us to concepts of faith in the final redemption. This is in fact the first record of classifying this cup as the cup of Eliyahu. It seems that the *Netziv* quoted above adopted this position and elucidated it further.

The *Aruch HaShulchan*[29] brings the minhag of the **Geonim** that only one who is very thirsty or sick can drink the fifth cup (as the Rema ruled), but concludes as follows: "However, we have never heard or seen such a thing that people act in such a manner." He then brings the opinion of Rabbeinu Yonah brought in the Tur and Rosh, that one is obligated to delve into the story of *yetziat mitzrayim* the entire night and tell of the wonders and miracles that Hashem did for us, and that if one drinks wine, he will fall asleep shortly thereafter. From the *Aruch HaShulchan's* formulation, it seems that he holds like Rabbeinu Yonah that not only is there no mitzva to drink the fifth cup, but there is also a prohibition.

Drinking from the Fifth Cup

Up to this point we haven't seen any of the *Acharonim* who states that one should drink the fifth cup. The *Tzitz Eliezer*[30] in his responsa quotes the following in the name of the *Ya'avetz*: "We prepare a big cup and we call it the cup of Eliyahu, but to drink from it, who ever mentioned that?" He continues that the *Ya'avetz* said that when he was with the *Chatam Sofer*, the cup for Eliyahu stood raised above all the other cups, but no one ever drank from it. The *Ya'avetz's* custom was to leave it out covered over the entire night, and in the morning to make *Kiddush* over it to fulfill the dictum of the Sages that since we have fulfilled one mitzva with it, we should use it for another.

Evidently, the *Chatam Sofer* never drank the fifth cup at all, while the *Ya'avetz* would only drink from it in the morning after reciting *Kiddush* over it. Perhaps the *Chatam Sofer* held like the *Netziv* that the fifth cup represents the final redemption and prophecy, and therefore would not drink from the cup at all, until the arrival of Eliyahu HaNavi and the renewal of prophecy.

However, the *Divrei Yetziv*[31] states in the name of the **Rokeach**[32] that we pour the fifth cup, recite *Hallel Hagadol*, and drink the fifth cup without leaning. He adds in the name of the *Manhig*[33] that the fifth cup is parallel to the expression "and I will bring you into the land" and is connected to the land.[34] The *Divrei Yetziv* concludes with the words of the Ra'avad[35] that "there is definitely what to rely on concerning this custom from the words of Rabbi Tarfon, and it is a mitzva to do as he says, and they have already connected this cup to the expression of *v'heveiti*. And even the *Tanna Kamma* stated

---

the fifth cup to the other four cups, which the *Chok Yaakov* does not do. Hence, we have presented the simple reading of his position as just pouring without drinking.

29. *Aruch HaShulchan*, o.c. 481:1–3.
30. Responsa *Tzitz Eliezer* 2:28.
31. Responsa *Divrei Yetziv*, o.c. 207 and 212.
32. Rokeach, *siman* 283.
33. *Sefer HaManhig*, *siman* 51.
34. This is also the opinion of the Ra'avad in his *Hasagot* on the Rif, as opposed to the *Netziv* who connected it to prophecy.
35. Ibid.

that one cannot drink less than four cups but regarding adding a cup, he did not say that it is prohibited." It seems that the *Divrei Yetziv* holds that one can and even should drink the fifth cup.

Concluding Thoughts

The **Maharal**[36] explains that the fifth cup focuses on *parnasa* (sustenance), which is an even higher level of redemption than *yetziat mitzrayim*. For although Hashem is above the Heavens, He still cares for each creature, giving them the sustenance they need. This care for each individual, explains the Maharal, is a more complete redemption and is signified by the fifth cup. This is also the theme of *Hallel Hagadol*, which on the one hand describes G-d's loftiness, yet also states, "He gives bread to all his creatures." The final redemption according to the Maharal will remove any deficiencies that we have.

Rav Shaar Yashuv HaKohen in his introduction to the *sefer zikaron* for his father, Rav David HaKohen (known as "The Nazir"),[37] recalls that his father, who waited for the return of prophecy all his life, said that this is the secret of the fifth cup, and when prophecy returns, we will once again have the custom to drink the fifth cup.

---

36. Maharal, *Sefer Gevurot Hashem, siman* 65.
37. Introduction to the book *"Ish ki Yafli".*

ERETZ HEMDAH
Institute for Advanced Jewish Studies
Jerusalem

Quito, Ecuador   קיטו, אקוודור

טבת תשנ"ג

נה. קיצור "ליל הסדר" לאנשים שאינם יודעים עברית

שאלה:

קהילתנו עומדת לארגן סדר פסח ציבורי לאנשי הקהילה. רוב האנשים לא יודעים לקרוא עברית, ולכן הייתי רוצה
לדעת האם יש אפשרות לקצר קטעים מסוימים מההגדה שהם לא מעכבים, או האם זה בלתי אפשרי?

תשובה:

אם לפי שיקול דעת הרב חשוב[1] להשמיט או לקצר[2] חלק מן ההגדה, אפשר לעשות כך בפיוטים של "נרצה"[3]. אין
להשמיט חלקים של "מגיד"[4], אבל אפשר לקרוא חלק נכבד מהם בלועזית[5] כדי להקל על המסובים ולהגביר את
ההתעניינות. את הקטעים שהם ברכות, פרקי הלל או מן התפילה (בסוף הלל) יש לומר בלשון הקודש[6]. כדאי להשאיר
את החלקים היותר ידועים בעברית, כדי לשמור על הטעם המיוחד של הסדר המסורתי.

---

[1] יש ענין חינוכי-פסיכולוגי בקריאת ההגדה המסורתית בשלימותה, כדי שלא ירגישו כאלו אין צריך ח"ו להתאמץ ולקיים
המצוות בשלימותן והידור, ורק במקום צורך גדול אפשר לקצר במקומות הפחות עיקריים.
[2] כגון לומר רק את הקטעים האחרונים המסכמים של "אחד מי יודע" או "חד גדיא".
[3] מזמורים אלה הם מאוחרים בהשוואה לשאר חלקי ההגדה ואינם מעיקר מצוות היום (סיפור יציאת מצריים, הלל, מצה, מרור
וד' כוסות).
[4] משום שזה עיקר סיפור יציאת מצרים.
[5] רמ"א או"ח סי' תעג, סעיף ו. פסקנו בעבר (ב"מראה הבזק" ח"א, ז, 2) שאין לומר את התפילה בלועזית באופן קבוע מג'
סיבות, וכולן לא שייכות כאן.
א. קשה לתרגם באופן השומר על הכוונה האמיתית של העניין - בסיפור יציאת מצריים אין מצוה מיוחדת על אמירת כל מלה.
המלים הן דרך להגיע ליעד של סיפור יציאת מצריים. בנדון דידן, אדרבה - סיפור יציאת מצרים יהיה יותר מושלם אם יאמרו
בשפה שמבינים. הרב א"י הכהן קוק זצ"ל כותב ב"אורח משפט" (סי' קכח ס"ק לד) : "יחייב כל אחד לדעת פירוש פשוט בהגדה
מתחילת 'עבדים היינו' עד 'הרי זה משובח' ולתרגם לבני ביתו שיבינו, ואחר כך 'מתחילה עובדי ע"ז' ויפסח מצה ומרור' ובכל
דור ודור חייב' עד ברכת 'גאל ישראל'.
ב. יש סגולות רבות בתפילה שנתקנה ע"י אנשי כנסת הגדולה, התלויות בלשון - סברא זאת שייכת במקצת גם כאן, אבל לא כמו
בתפילה, שהרי "מגיד" הוא ליקוט של מאמרי חז"ל שלא נכתבו מלכתחילה כדי לצרפם לסדר פסח.
ג. מסוכן לשנות את התפילה בגלל כניעה לזרם הריפורמיים – אולם בהגדה, שעיקר תקנתה הוא העברת המסר ולא הנוסח
המדויק, לא מורגשת הקריאה בלועזית כל כך כשינוי מהותי של המנהג הקדום. נוסף על כך, כבר מקובל מדורי דורות בחוגים
של יראים ושלמים לתרגם קטעים שלמים של ההגדה ללועזית (מה שלא היה נהוג בתפילה). על-פי הצעתנו ישארו חלקים של ההגדה
בלשון הקודש, והמקור לא ישכח אפוא לגמרי.
[6] עיין בנימוקים ביחס לתפילה בהערה 5.

3

Hilchot Leil Haseder II
הלכות ליל הסדר ב׳

Maror

Korech

Shulchan Orech

Tzafun

Barech

Hallel

Nirtza

For quick reference, some long website URLs have been shortened.
For the complete list of referenced websites visit www.tzurbaolami.com.

ת	**Tanach**	
ח	**Talmud (Chazal)**	
ר	*Rishonim*	
א	*Acharonim*	
◆	**Contemporary Halachic Sources**	

In the previous *shiur*, we studied halachic issues related to the Seder through the section of *motzee-matza*. In Part Two, we will continue with the *halachot* related to the next stage of the Seder, the eating of the *maror*, through the completion of the Seder.

MAROR

There is a Torah obligation to eat the *korban pesach* (Paschal offering) together with matza and *maror* (bitter herbs).

Shemot 12:8	**1. שמות	יב:ח**

They shall eat the flesh that same night; they shall eat it roasted over the fire, with unleavened bread and with bitter herbs.

וְאָכְלוּ אֶת הַבָּשָׂר בַּלַּיְלָה הַזֶּה צְלִי אֵשׁ וּמַצּוֹת עַל מְרֹרִים יֹאכְלֻהוּ:

It is clear from the above verse that the consumption of *maror* is an integral part of the mitzva to eat the *korban pesach*. Therefore, the Gemara explains that when the *korban pesach* is no longer offered, the mitzva of *maror* applies by rabbinic law only, in contrast to matza, for which there is an additional verse that records the obligation to eat it independently.

Masechet Pesachim 120a	**2. מסכת פסחים קכ.**

Rava said: The mitzva of ***matza*** **nowadays,** even after the destruction of the Temple, applies by **Torah** law; **but** the mitzva to eat **bitter herbs** applies **by rabbinic law. And** in **what** way **are bitter herbs different from** *matza*? **As it is written,** with regard to the Paschal offering: "They shall eat it **with** *matzot* **and bitter herbs**" (*Bamidbar* 9:11), from which it is derived: **When there is** an obligation to eat **the Paschal offering, there is** likewise a mitzva to eat **bitter herbs; and when there is no** obligation to eat

אמר רבא: מצה בזמן הזה דאורייתא ומרור דרבנן. ומאי שנא מרור דכתיב על מצות ומרורים בזמן דאיכא פסח – יש מרור, ובזמן דליכא פסח – ליכא מרור. מצה נמי הא כתיב על מצות ומרורים! – מצה מיהדר הדר ביה קרא בערב תאכלו מצת.

the Paschal offering, there is also **no** mitzva to eat **bitter herbs.** But if so, the same reasoning should apply to *matza* **as well,** as **it is written:** "**With** *matzot* **and bitter herbs.**" The Gemara rejects this contention: **The verse repeats** the obligation to eat *matza*: "In the first month, on the fourteenth day of the month **in the evening, you shall eat** *matzot*" (*Shemot* 12:18).

The **Rambam** rules in accordance with the above passage in the Gemara:

⬠ Rambam, Hilchot Chametz Umatza 7:12

Eating the *maror* is not an independent Torah obligation. Rather, it is dependent upon the consumption of the *korban pesach*. For there is one positive commandment to eat the meat of the *korban pesach* together with matzah and *maror*, and by rabbinic law, [one is obligated] to eat *maror* by itself on this night, even if there is no *korban pesach*.

3. רמב"ם | הל' חמץ ומצה ז:יב

אכילת מרור אינה מצוה מן התורה בפני עצמה אלא תלויה היא באכילת הפסח, שמצות עשה אחת לאכול בשר הפסח על מצה ומרורים, ומדברי סופרים לאכול המרור לבדו בליל זה אפילו אין שם קרבן פסח.

Although it is only a rabbinic mitzva, the *beracha* "who sanctified us with his commandments and commanded us regarding the eating of *maror* [*al achilat maror*]" is still recited.

Which Species Are Defined as *Maror*?

The Mishna in *Masechet Pesachim* (2:6) lists different species of vegetables that qualify as *maror*. The **Gemara** clarifies that among all the species listed in the Mishna, the ideal one to use in fulfilling the mitzva is the *chazeret*.

⬡ Masechet Pesachim 39a

And Rabbi Oshaya said: The optimal fulfillment of the mitzva is **with *chazeret*, and Rava said: What is *chazeret*?** It is **lettuce [*chassa*].**

The Gemara explains: **What is** the meaning of **lettuce [*chassa*]?** It refers to the fact **that God has mercy [*chas*] on us.**

4. מסכת פסחים לט.

ואמר רבי אושעיא: מצוה בחזרת. ואמר רבא: מאי חזרת – חסא. מאי חסא – דחס רחמנא עילוון.

According to the Gemara, the term *chazeret* refers to lettuce, which the *poskim* confirm is in fact the romaine lettuce with which we are familiar today. The ***Shulchan Aruch*** rules in accordance with the Gemara that the ideal manner of fulfilling the mitzva of *maror* is by eating lettuce.

א Shulchan Aruch, Orach Chaim 473:5

These are the vegetables with which one can fulfill one's obligation... and the primary mitzva is with *chazeret* [i.e., lettuce].

5. שולחן ערוך | או"ח תעג:ה

אלו ירקות שיוצאים בהם ידי חובתו... ועיקר המצוה בחזרת.

In modern times, the question has arisen that the taste of romaine lettuce does not appear to be particularly bitter, and sometimes lettuce even tastes a bit sweet. The reason for this is that lettuce today is grown in such a manner that during the earlier stages of its growth, it is somewhat sweet, while in its later stages it becomes bitter. The lettuce is generally harvested before it has completely finished growing in order to preserve the sweetness. If so, can one fulfill one's obligation with such lettuce?

The *poskim* in fact dispute whether it is sufficient to simply use a species defined as *maror* or must one be capable of actually tasting the bitterness. According to the ***Chazon Ish***, this type of lettuce is invalid for fulfilling the mitzva. He understood that one must actually taste the bitterness, and therefore the lettuce used for *maror* must be harvested at a later stage of growth.

 Chazon Ish, Hilchot Pesach, Siman 124, Pesachim 39a

6. חזון איש | הל' פסח, סימן קכד, פסחים לט.

The main usage of lettuce [today] is before it becomes bitter, and the *chazeret* commonly spoken about and used by people is the sweet one. Therefore, it is logical that it isn't included in the *maror* [required] by the verse. Now the *Chacham Tzvi* writes that it [*chazeret*] is "salad" in the vernacular [i.e., lettuce], but one must be careful not to fulfill the mitzva with it until it has become bitter, but in the end it is as bitter as wormwood, as the *Chacham Tzvi* has written. So one must pick it before it becomes bitter to this extent.[1]

דעיקר שימוש החזרת הוא קודם שהומרר וחזרת שנקרא בפיות בני אדם ושמשמין בו הוא המתוק ולפיכך מסתבר שאינו בכלל מרורים דקרא, והנה החכם צבי כתב דהוא סאלאט בלע"ז (חסה של ימינו) וצריך ליזהר שלא לצאת בו עד שיתמרר ובסופו הוא מר כלענה, כמו שכתב החכם צבי וצריך ליקח קודם שיתמרר כל כך.

Some have the custom to use horseradish as *maror* or to place a bit of horseradish together with the lettuce used for *korech* in order to taste the bitterness, in compliance with this opinion of the *Chazon Ish*. However, most *poskim* hold that one can fulfill one's obligation with lettuce even if it is slightly sweet and not bitter, as the determining factor is that it is defined as a *maror* vegetable. They cite proof for this position from the following passage in the *Talmud Yerushalmi*.

Talmud Yerushalmi, Pesachim 2:5

7. תלמוד ירושלמי | פסחים ב:ה

Just as *chazeret* is sweet in the beginning and bitter in the end, so did the Egyptians do to our forefathers: In the beginning [they said], "in the choice of the land place your father and brothers" (*Bereishit* 47:6), and in the end "they embittered their lives with hard work" (*Shemot* 1:14).

מה חזרת תחילתה מתוק וסופה מר, כך עשו המצריים לאבותינו במצרים, בתחילה 'במיטב הארץ הושב את אביך ואת אחיך' (בראשית מז:ו), ואחר כך 'וימררו את חייהם בעבודה קשה' (שמות א:יד).

It seems from the *Yerushalmi* that although the *chazeret* is initially sweet and only later becomes bitter, it is still defined as *maror*, and in fact it is specifically this species that is chosen as the ideal one for fulfilling the mitzva. This position is adopted by the **Shulchan Aruch Harav** in addition to other *Acharonim*.

א **Shulchan Aruch HaRav, Orach Chaim 473**

8. שולחן ערוך הרב | או"ח תעג

Even though *chazeret* has no bitterness, nevertheless when it is in the ground, the stem hardens and becomes bitter. For this reason, it is called *maror*, and it is a mitzva to look for it even though it is sweet.

ואע"פ שהחזרת אין בה מרירות, מכל מקום כשהוא בקרקע מתקשה הקלח ונעשה מר מאוד ומפני כך נקרא מרור ומצוה לחזר אחריה אף כשהיא מתוקה.

---

1. The *Chazon Ish* means that on one hand, one may not use romaine lettuce that was picked at an earlier stage of growth when it is not yet bitter. On the other hand, if one waits too long, then it gets excessively bitter and is inedible. Rather, the lettuce must be at a stage of growth in between these two extremes. See also the *Dirshu* edition of the *Mishna Berura*, *siman* 473, 56 and the additional sources quoted there. [Addition of the English editors]

RABBI SHNEUR ZALMAN OF LIADI – THE BA'AL HATANYA (1745–1812)

Rav Shneur Zalman of Liadi was the founder and first head of the Chabad-Lubavitch movement. He was born in Liozna (present-day Belarus) to descendants of the Maharal of Prague. Even as a child, he displayed extraordinary prowess, writing a commentary on the Torah based on Rashi, Ramban, and Ibn Ezra at the age of eight. He married at age fifteen and then proceeded to become a student of Rav Dov Ber of Mezeritch, the Chassidic leader known as the Maggid of Mezeritch. During the next few years, he studied classic Talmudic material, in addition to philosophy, Kabbala, and Chassidut, and even some secular disciplines such as mathematics and astronomy. Rav Shneur Zalman later became one of the leaders of the Chassidic movement in general, and founded the Chabad branch of the movement as well. The Chabad movement was distinguished by its intellectual approach to Chassidic and Kabbalistic ideas. His classic work *Tanya* (by which he is often referred to as the *Ba'al HaTanya*) was geared toward just such an intellectual understanding and is studied by many today including those not affiliated with Chabad or even the overall Chassidic movement.

He also wrote the halachic work known as the *Shulchan Aruch HaRav,* written in the order and in the style of the *Shulchan Aruch,* but which also provides many of the rulings and customs followed by the Chabad movement today. This work is considered a classic in halachic literature, and is widely quoted by many other important *poskim,* including the *Mishna Berura, Aruch HaShulchan,* and *Ben Ish Chai.*

Rav Shneur Zalman was falsely accused of treason (possibly based on accusations made by the non-Chassidic Lithuanian Jewish community) in 1798 and imprisoned as a result for fifty-three days. His release, which took place on the Hebrew date of the 19th of Kislev, is celebrated as a holiday by Chabad Chassidim, and in recent years has evolved as a general celebration of the greatness of Chassidut. Following his release, he moved to Liadi, where he continued to develop the Chabad movement. Following his death, his son became the leader of Chabad and relocated the movement's headquarters to the town of Lubavitch (Lyubavichi, in present day Russia), the name by which the movement is still known today.

One of the proofs of the *Chazon Ish* to his opinion is the halacha (cited later in this *shiur*) that one shouldn't leave the *maror* in the *charoset* for too long in order not to nullify the taste of the *maror*. The *Chazon Ish* opines that this is a conclusive proof that the taste is a critical element in fulfilling the mitzva.

However, **Rav Asher Weiss** argues that there is no need to actually taste the bitterness. Rather, one is obligated to eat the *maror* in a manner that would allow one to taste any bitterness potentially found therein. Therefore, one shouldn't actively do anything that would negate the possibility of being able to taste the bitterness.

 Minchat Asher, Haggada Shel Pesach p. 202

9. מנחת אשר | הגדה של פסח עמ' רב

In truth, it is a great novelty to say that [not] being able to taste the flavor can prevent one from fulfilling the mitzva, for "eating" is written in the Torah, so from where would we know to add this novelty that taste is an intrinsic part of the mitzva? In truth it seems that there is no need to taste the flavor of the *maror*; rather one has to eat it in a manner that one would be able to taste the bitter flavor... for there is no specific definition for what is called bitter, since that which is bitter for one person is not bitter for another person, as is known...

דבאמת חידוש הוא לומר דהרגשת הטעם מעכבת במצוה, והלא בתורה אכילה כתיב, ומניין לחדש שהרגשת הטעם הוא מעיקרי המצווה, ונראה דבאמת אין צריך להרגיש טעם המרור אלא דצריך לאכול אותו באופן הראוי להרגיש בו טעמו המר... דאין זה דבר מסוים מה נקרא מר, ומה שמר לפלוני אינו מר לאלמוני כידוע...

The Manner in Which to Eat the *Maror*

In order to fulfill the mitzva of *maror*, one must eat a *kezayit* (olive-size) of it. The **Sefer Yere'im** explains whenever the Torah mentions the word eating (*achila*), the measurement must be at least a *kezayit*. This halacha therefore applies to *maror*, about which it is written "they shall eat it with matzot and *maror*."

Sefer Yere'im, Siman 94 | 10. ספר יראים | סימן צד

One must eat a *kezayit* of *maror*, as "eating" is written regarding it, and eating [is defined] as a *kezayit*.

וצריך שיאכל מן המרור כזית דאכילה כתיב ביה ואכילה בכזית.

Therefore, it is recommended to measure the pieces of lettuce that one intends to use at the Seder on Erev Pesach to ensure that everyone eats a *kezayit* without complication.

As opposed to other foods at the Seder, one does not recline while eating *maror*, as evident from the **Gemara** below.

Masechet Pesachim 108a | 11. מסכת פסחים קח.

It was stated: **Matza needs** to be eaten while **reclining**, *maror* **does not need to be.**

איתמר: מצה – צריך הסיבה, מרור – אין צריך.

Rashi, Pesachim 108a | 12. רש"י | פסחים קח.

Maror does not need reclining – For this is in commemoration of the slavery.

מרור אין צריך הסיבה – שהוא זכר לעבדות.

The **Shulchan Aruch** codifies the halacha of eating *maror* as follows:

Shulchan Aruch, Orach Chaim 475:1 | 13. שולחן ערוך | או"ח תעה:א

And one recites the *beracha* of "*al achilat maror*" and eats it without reclining.

ויברך על אכילת מרור ויאכלנו בלא הסיבה.

One should dip the *maror* in *charoset* before eating it, but then shake off the *charoset* from the *maror*, as described by the **Shulchan Aruch**.

Shulchan Aruch, Ibid. | 14. שולחן ערוך | שם

Afterwards, one takes a *kezayit* of *maror* and immerses it in *charoset*, but one should not leave it inside, in order not to nullify the bitterness. And for this reason, one shakes off the *charoset* from it.

ואחר כך יקח כזית מרור וישקענו כולו בחרוסת, ולא ישהנו בתוכו שלא יבטל טעם מרירותו ומטעם זה צריך לנער החרוסת מעליו.

Mishna Berura 475:13

And immerses it – In order to kill the poison in it.[2] There are some places where the custom is not to immerse it entirely; rather they dip it slightly.

15. משנה ברורה | תעה:יג

וישקענו כולו – כדי להמית ארס שבתוכו. ויש מקומות שאין נוהגין לשקע כולו אלא בטיבול מקצתו.

The *beracha* of *borei pri ha'adama* is not recited over the *maror*. Two reasons are given for this.

Tosafot, Pesachim 115a

It seems that one doesn't need to recite *borei pri ha'adama,* even though the *Haggada* is considered an interruption, as explained previously, and one wouldn't be exempt with the *beracha* on the first dipping [i.e., *Karpas*]. Nevertheless, the *beracha* of *hamotzee* exempts it, as it is considered foods that are brought within the meal due to the meal, since vegetables are an appetizer [lit. they drag the heart].

16. תוספות | פסחים קטו.

נראה דאין צריך לברך בפה"א אף על גב דהגדה הוי הפסק כדפרישית לעיל ולא מיפטר בברכה של טיבול ראשון מ"מ ברכת המוציא פוטרתן דהוה להו דברים הבאים בתוך הסעודה מחמת הסעודה שהרי ירקות גוררין הלב.

Rosh, Pesachim 10:26

The Rashbam explains that one doesn't need to recite *borei pri ha'adama* because one has already been exempted with the *beracha* that one recited over the vegetables [*Karpas*].

17. רא"ש | פסחים י:כו

ופי' רשב"ם ואין צריך לברך בורא פרי האדמה לפי שנפטר בברכה שבירך על הירקות.

According to **Tosafot**, the *beracha* recited previously during *Karpas* is not effective for the *maror,* since the *Haggada* interrupts in between. But Tosafot hold that the *maror* is included in the *beracha* over bread, since it does serve a function related to the meal. According to the **Rosh** citing the **Rashbam**, the *beracha* recited during Karpas is effective for the *maror,* and apparently the *Haggada* is not considered an interruption since it is all part of the Seder. Nevertheless, both agree that as mentioned no *beracha* is recited on the *maror.*

---

2. According to the Gemara (*Pesachim* 115a), one of the reasons for dipping the *maror* in the *charoset* is that the *maror* may contain some sort of poisonous substance, which the *charoset* nullifies. Although people eat *maror* vegetables the rest of the year without *charoset,* the Rosh explains that the Sages did not want to risk any harm befalling someone due to the performance of a mitzva. [Addition of the English editors]

KORECH

In order to understand the correct procedure to follow for *Korech*, we need to first examine a passage in the Gemara in *Pesachim*, which cites the dispute between the Rabbis and Hillel as to how the matza and *maror* were eaten during Temple times.

| ח | Masechet Pesachim 115a | 18. מסכת פסחים קטו. | ח |

They said about Hillel that he would wrap *matza* and bitter herbs **together and eat them, as it is stated: "They shall eat it with *matzot* and bitter herbs"** (*Bamidbar* 9:11), which indicates that these two foods should be consumed together.

Rabbi Yochanan said: Hillel's **colleagues disagree with him, as it was taught** in another *beraita*: I **might** have thought that **one** should **wrap** *matzot* and bitter herbs **together and eat them in the manner that Hillel eats them;** therefore **the verse states: "They shall eat it with *matzot* and bitter herbs,"** meaning that one may eat **even this,** the *matza,* **by itself, and that,** the bitter herbs, **by themselves.**

אמרו עליו על הלל שהיה כורכן בבת אחת ואוכלן שנאמר: "על מצות ומרורים יאכלוהו." אמר רבי יוחנן חולקין עליו חביריו על הלל דתניא יכול יהא כורכן בבת אחת ואוכלן כדרך שהלל אוכלן תלמוד לומר על מצות ומרורים יאכלוהו אפילו זה בפני עצמו וזה בפני עצמו.

According to the Gemara, the Rabbis and Hillel disagree as to whether the matza and *maror* were eaten together with the *korban pesach* or separately: Hillel holds that they were to be eaten together, while the Rabbis hold that they were to be eaten separately.

There is no conclusive ruling about this dispute, and the Gemara cited below, in the continuation of the same passage, states that one should follow both opinions. Therefore, we first eat the matza and *maror* separately and then during *Korech* we eat them together in accordance with the opinion of Hillel.

| ח | Ibid. | שם. 19 | ח |

Now that the *halacha* was stated neither in accordance with the opinion of **Hillel nor in accordance with** the opinion of **the Rabbis,** one **recites the blessing:** Commanded us over **eating matza, and eats** *matza* to fulfill his obligation. **And then he recites the blessing:** Commanded us **over eating *maror*, and eats. And then he eats** *matza* **and lettuce together without a blessing in remembrance of the Temple, in the manner of Hillel** in the days of the Temple.

השתא דלא איתמר הלכתא לא כהלל ולא כרבנן מברך על אכילת מצה ואכיל, והדר מברך על אכילת מרור ואכיל, והדר אכיל מצה וחסא בהדי הדדי בלא ברכה זכר למקדש כהלל.

Since our performance of *Korech* is designed to commemorate the opinion of Hillel, who held that one must eat the matza and *maror* together to fulfill the mitzva, it is logical that all of the *halachot* that apply to eating matza and *maror* individually should also apply with regard to *Korech*, e.g., eating a *kezayit* of matza and *maror*, as well as dipping the *maror* into *charoset*. This is indeed the ruling of the **Shulchan Aruch**:

א Shulchan Aruch, Orach Chaim 475:1

20. שולחן ערוך | או"ח תעה:א

Afterwards one takes the third matza and breaks it and makes a sandwich with the *maror*, and dips it in the *charoset*. One says [the paragraph of] *zecher lemikdash k'Hillel* (a commemoration of the Temple in accordance with Hillel). Then one eats them together while reclining. From the time that one recites the *beracha* of *al achilat matza*, one must not interrupt with any matter that is not related to the meal until he eats this sandwich, in order that the *beracha* of *al achilat matza* and the *beracha* of *al achilat maror* apply also to the sandwich.

ואחר כך נוטל מצה שלישית ובוצע ממנה וכורכה עם המרור וטובלה בחרוסת ואומר זכר למקדש כהלל ואוכלן ביחד בהסיבה ומשיברך על אכילת מצה לא יסיח בדבר שאינו מענין הסעודה עד שיאכל כריכה זו כדי שתעלה ברכת אכילת מצה וברכת אכילת מרור גם לכריכה זו.

In summary: On the Seder night, one must eat two measures of a *kezayit* of *maror* (lettuce), one independently during the stage of *Maror* and one during *Korech* together with the matza.

SHULCHAN ORECH

During the period of the Mishna, some had the custom not to eat roasted meat on the Seder night as it might appear as if they were eating the *korban pesach* outside of the Temple complex. Others though were accustomed to eating roasted meat provided they did not eat an entire lamb, as documented by the Mishna below.

ח	Mishna, Pesachim 4:4	.21 משנה | פסחים ד:ד

In a place where the custom is to eat roasted meat on Seder night, one may eat. In a place where the custom is not to eat, one may not eat.

מקום שנהגו לאכול צלי בלילי פסחים – אוכלין. מקום שנהגו שלא לאכול – אין אוכלין.

The **Shulchan Aruch** quotes this ruling of the Mishna.

א	Shulchan Aruch, Orach Chaim 476:1	.22 שולחן ערוך | או"ח תעו:א

In a place where they were accustomed to eat roasted meat on the Seder night, it is permitted to eat. In a place where the custom is not to eat, one may not eat as a rabbinic decree lest others [mistakenly] say that it is meat from the *korban pesach*.

מקום שנהגו לאכול צלי בלילי פסחים אוכלים. מקום שנהגו שלא לאכול אין אוכלין גזירה שמא יאמרו בשר פסח הוא.

The common custom among both Sephardim and Ashkenazim is not to eat roasted meat on the Seder night (see **Mishna Berura** 476:1; **Chazon Ovadia** Vol. 2, p. 103). However, the custom is limited to the Seder night only, but during the day, it is permitted to eat roasted meat, as stated below.

	Chazon Ovadia, Pesach Vol. 2, p. 104	.23 חזון עובדיה | פסח חלק ב, עמ' קד

During the daytime Pesach meal, it is permitted to eat even the roasted meat of the foreleg, as the concern was only for the night of Pesach, which is the appropriate time for eating the *korban pesach*, as opposed to the day of Pesach.

בסעודת היום של פסח, מותר לאכול אף מבשר הזרוע שהוא צלי, שלא חששו אלא בליל פסח שהוא זמן אכילת קרבן פסח, מה שאין כן ביום חג הפסח.

With regard to the nighttime custom, the **Mishna Berura** adds that pot-roast and meat roasted after being cooked are also included within the custom.

א | **Mishna Berura 476:1**   **24. משנה ברורה | תעו:א**

Even pot-roast [*tzli kedar*] (i.e., it is roasted in a pot without water or any other liquid, but cooks in its own juices), even though it is not similar to the roasting of the *korban pesach*, for the *pesach* roasted in a pot is invalid; nevertheless it should be prohibited due to *marit ayin* (the appearance of a prohibition), so that people don't err and also permit a regular roast. And even if it was originally cooked in water and made into pot-roast only afterwards, one should prohibit it for the same reason.

ואפילו צלי קדר [פי' שנצלה בקדירה בלא מים ושום משקה אלא מתבשל במוהל היוצא ממנו] אף על פי שאינו דומה לצליית הפסח שהפסח שנצלה בקדירה פסול אפ"ה יש לאוסרו מפני מראית העין שלא יטעו להתיר גם צלי אש ואפילו אם בישלו מתחלה במים ואח"כ עשאו צלי קדר יש לאסור מטעם זה.

The **Rema** cites the custom of eating eggs at the beginning of the meal and offers two reasons for it.

א | **Rema, Orach Chaim 476:2**   **25. רמ"א | או"ח תעו:ב**

The custom in some places is to eat eggs during the meal as a remembrance for the mourning [of the Temple].[3] It seems to me that the reason is that the night of Tisha B'av has been established [according to the calendar as being] the [same] night [of the week] as the night of Pesach, and furthermore as a remembrance for the Temple, where the *korban pesach* was brought.

נוהגים בקצת מקומות לאכול בסעודה ביצים זכר לאבילות ונראה לי הטעם משום שליל תשעה באב נקבע בליל פסח ועוד זכר לחורבן שהיו מקריבין קרבן פסח.

The **Vilna Gaon** disagreed with the reasons suggested by the Rema for this custom. In his opinion, one should certainly not do anything as a sign of mourning on Pesach. Rather, he explains that eggs commemorate the *korban chagiga* (festival offering brought on the three Festivals).

א | **Ma'aseh Rav, Hilchot Pesach 191**   **26. מעשה רב | הל' פסח קצא**

After that we eat the egg. The reason for this is not due to mourning, for Heaven forbid that we should recall mourning of Tisha B'av on this day. Rather, it is in order to commemorate the *korban chagiga*, for one cannot eat roast on Pesach night. Instead, we eat [non-roasted] meat in commemoration of the *korban pesach* and the egg in commemoration of the *korban chagiga*.

ואחר כך אוכלין הביצה וטעם האכילה לא מפני אבילות, כי חס וחלילה להזכיר אבילות תשעה באב היום, רק הטעם שהוא זכר לחגיגה, כי צלי אין לאכול בפסח, רק בשר זכר לפסח וביצה זכר לחגיגה.

The *poskim* note that one must be careful not to become too full during the meal, since one must still have an appetite to eat the *afikoman*.

א | **Rema, Orach Chaim 476:2**   **27. רמ"א | או"ח תעו:ב**

One should not eat or drink excessively so that one does not consume the *afikoman* in a state of gluttony or become drunk and fall asleep immediately.

ולא יאכל ולא ישתה הרבה יותר מדאי שלא יאכל האפיקומן על אכילה גסה או ישתכר וישן מיד.

---

3.   Eggs are often viewed as a sign of mourning, and are also served at the first meal of a mourner at his home after the death and burial of a relative. The reason for this is that eggs are round, symbolizing the cycle of life that includes birth as well as death (*Shibolei HaLeket, Hilchot Aveilut*). [Addition of the English editors]

TZAFUN

Following *Shulchan Orech*, it is time for the eating of the *afikoman*, which is referred to as *Tzafun*, meaning concealed (since it was concealed until now). The name *afikoman* comes from the Mishna in *Pesachim*, which states that one may not eat any *afikoman* following the consumption of the *korban pesach*. According to the Gemara, it is a play on the Aramaic words *afiku man*, "bring out the sweets." The **Gemara** then continues to define the types of foods included in this prohibition in the passage below:

☝ Masechet Pesachim 119b	28. מסכת פסחים קיט:

MISHNA: One does not conclude after the Paschal offering with an *afikoman*.

GEMARA: The Gemara asks: **What** is the meaning of ***afikoman*?** ...**Rabbi Yochanan** says: *afikoman* refers to foods **such as dates, roasted grains, and nuts,** which are eaten during the meal. It **was taught** in a *beraita* **in accordance with** the opinion of **Rabbi Yochanan: One does not conclude** by eating foods **such as dates, roasted grains, and nuts after the *korban pesach*.**

משנה: אין מפטירין אחר הפסח אפיקומן.

גמרא: מאי אפיקומן? ...רבי יוחנן אמר כגון תמרים קליות ואגוזים תניא כוותיה דרבי יוחנן אין מפטירין אחר הפסח כגון תמרים קליות ואגוזים.

This prohibition of eating following the *korban pesach* is still relevant today, even though we unfortunately do not offer the *korban pesach*. The reason is that we eat matza at the conclusion of the meal in place of the *korban pesach*. This matza has come to be known by the name "*afikoman*." Therefore, one may not eat anything afterwards that will remove the taste of the matza.

The *Rishonim* dispute which *kezayit* of matza fulfills the obligation of the biblical mitzva of eating matza (from "in the evening you shall eat matza"), the *kezayit* eaten at the beginning of the meal for *motzee-matza* or the matza used for *afikoman* at the end of the meal. **Rashi** holds that the obligation refers to the matza used for the *afikoman*. Nevertheless, we still recite the *beracha* of "*al achilat matza*" during *motzee-matza*.

☝ Rashi, Pesachim 119b	29. רש"י	פסחים קיט:

One does not conclude after the matza with an *afikoman* – For one needs to eat matza at the end of the meal in commemoration of the matza that was eaten together with the *korban pesach*.[4] This is the broken matza that we eat at the end to fulfill our obligation of eating matza after the meal. But we are forced to recite the *beracha* of *al achilat matza* at the beginning, [even though it is not] for the obligation,

אין מפטירין אחר מצה אפיקומן – שצריך לאכול מצה בגמר הסעודה זכר למצה הנאכלת עם הפסח, וזו היא מצה הבצועה שאנו אוכלין באחרונה לשם חובת מצה אותה שלאחר אכילה, ועל כרחינו אנו מברכין על אכילת מצה בראשונה, [אף על פי שאינה באה] לשם חובה,

---

4. Rashi's explanation here is somewhat difficult to understand, as here he writes that the matza is "in commemoration of the matza that was eaten together with the *korban pesach*," while below he writes that this matza fulfills the biblical obligation for eating matza on the night of Pesach. Perhaps he means that we intend for the consumption of this matza alone to fulfill the biblical obligation (and not the matza eaten earlier), but the reason we eat it after the meal and not before is that it commemorates the matza that was eaten with the *korban pesach* during Temple times.

as Rav Chisda stated earlier (*Pesachim* 115a) regarding *maror* that after one has filled his stomach with it, how can he then recite a *beracha* on it? The same is true concerning matza…

כדאמר רב חסדא לעיל (פסחים קטו, א) גבי מרור דלאחר שמילא כריסו הימנו היאך חוזר ומברך עליו, הכי נמי גבי מצה...

Other *Rishonim*, such as the **Rashbam** and **Kol Bo**, also agree with Rashi.[5] By contrast, the **Rosh** and **Ramban** (*Milchemet Hashem* on *Pesachim* 119b) hold that the obligation of matza refers to the first matza eaten during *motzee-matza*, as if the *afikoman* were indeed the obligation, it should have been eaten with *maror* and *charoset*. Therefore, they explain that the eating of the *afikoman* matza is just in commemoration for the *korban pesach*.

🏠 Rosh, Pesachim 10:34 | .30 רא"ש | פסחים י:לד

According to this [the opinion of Rashi] it would seem that one should also eat *maror* and *charoset* with it, since it is a remembrance of the matza that was eaten with the *pesach* in a sandwich… however, [if so] I am astounded as to why we would make a sandwich at the beginning [of the meal], surely one at the end as a remembrance for the Temple should suffice? Therefore, it seems to me that the matza [at the end] is not for the sake of the obligation. Rather it is eaten as a remembrance for the *korban pesach*, which was eaten at the end of the meal when one was sated. Since it is a remembrance for the *korban pesach*, it receives the laws of the *pesach* not to eat afterwards.

ולפי זה (שיטת רש"י) היה נראה שצריך לאכול עמה מרור וחרוסת כיון שהיא זכר מצה הנאכלת עם הפסח בכריכה... אמנם תמיהני למה עושין כריכה בתחילה יספיק בכריכה אחרונה זכר למקדש הלכך נראה לי דאותה מצה אינה לשם חובה אלא אוכלין אותה זכר לפסח שהיה נאכל על השובע באחרונה ולפי שהוא זכר לפסח יש ליתן לה דין הפסח שלא לאכול אחריה.

A third approach to the significance of the *afikoman* is offered by **Tosafot** and the **Ritva** (*Hilchot Seder Haggada*). They hold that the Sages instituted the eating of the *afikoman* in order that the taste of matza remain in our mouths as an expression of endearment of the mitzva, similar to the halacha concerning the *korban pesach*.

🏠 Tosafot, Pesachim 120a | .31 תוספות | פסחים קכ.

…It is good to eat it while sated and for the flavor of the matza to remain in one's mouth. But if he has enough matza for the entire meal he should eat matza at the beginning of the meal with an appetite and recite the *beracha* over it. Afterwards, at the end of the meal one should eat [another] *kezayit* of matza and the taste of the matza will remain in one's mouth. But the primary mitzva is [fulfilled] with the first one, which is eaten with an appetite, and one will also have the taste of matza in his mouth at the end [of the meal] with the last *kezayit*…

...דטוב לאוכלו על השובע ולהיות טעם מצה בפיו אבל ודאי אי אית ליה מצה לכל סעודתו טוב לו לאכול מצה בתחלה לתיאבון ולברך עליה ואח"כ בגמר סעודתו יאכל כזית מצה ויהיה טעם מצה בפיו ועיקר מצוה על הראשונה שהיא באה לתיאבון וגם יהא לבסוף טעם מצה בפיו באותו כזית אחרון...

---

5. The Rambam's opinion about this issue is unclear, as he states the following (*Hilchot Chametz Umatza* 8:9): "And then the meal continues, and he eats whatever he wishes to eat and drinks whatever he wishes to drink, and at the end he eats at least a *kezayit* from the meat of the *pesach* and may not taste anything afterwards. And nowadays he eats a *kezayit* of matza and does not taste anything afterwards, so that it should be the end of the meal, and the taste of the meat of the *pesach* or the matza is in his mouth, as their consumption is the mitzva." From the last phrase it appears that the Rambam agrees with Rashi, as noted by the *Aruch HaShulchan* (477:2). However, this is not conclusive; see note below.

To summarize, there are three opinions regarding the reason for eating the *afikoman*:

1. Eating this matza fulfills the obligation of "in the evening you shall eat matza" (Rashi; Rashbam)
2. The *afikoman* commemorates the *korban pesach* (Ramban; Rosh)
3. The *afikoman* is simply a means to retain the flavor of matza in one's mouth (Tosafot; Ritva)

There are a number of practical ramifications to this dispute, such as whether one needs to eat while reclining (see footnote).[6]

The Amount That Needs to Be Eaten

Logically, it would seem that one must eat a *kezayit* of matza for *afikoman*, similar to other mitzvot of eating where a *kezayit* is required. This is apparent as well from the words of the **Rambam** (*Chametz Umatza* 8:9) and the majority of *Rishonim*.

However, the **Maharal** (*Seder Haggada* 38) writes that since the mitzva of matza is such a special mitzva, one should eat two *kezayit* portions. This is also the opinion of the **Bach**, albeit for a different reason. He opines that one should eat two *kezayit* portions since *Rishonim* dispute whether the *afikoman* commemorates the *korban pesach* or the matzah that was eaten with it. Therefore, one should fulfill both opinions by eating two portions.

א Bayit Chadash (Bach), Orach Chaim 477	32. בית חדש (ב"ח) | או"ח תעז

Our custom is to take the bigger portion for the *afikoman*... and we eat the amount of two *kezayit* portions from it, one in remembrance of the *korban pesach* as the Rosh writes, and one in remembrance of the matzah that was eaten with the *pesach*, as the Rashbam explains... Now since according to the Rosh this eating is only in remembrance of the *korban pesach* and not for the sake of the obligation to eat matza, and according to the Rashbam it is for the obligation of matza that is eaten with the *pesach*, we therefore need [to eat] two *kezayit* portions, and one doesn't suffice, in order to remove oneself from this dispute.

ומנהגינו ליקח חלק הגדול לאפיקומן... ואוכלין ממנו כשיעור שני זיתים – אחד זכר לפסח כאשר כתב הרא"ש ואחד זכר למצה הנאכלת עם הפסח כאשר פירש רשב"ם... ומשום דלהרא"ש אין אכילה זו אלא זכר לפסח ולא לשם חובת אכילת מצה ולפירוש רשב"ם היא משום חובת מצה הנאכלת עם הפסח על כן צריך שני זיתים ולא סגי כזית אחד לאפוקי נפשיה מפלוגתא.

The **Shulchan Aruch** rules that one must eat only one *kezayit* for the *afikoman* at the end of the meal, but the **Mishna Berura** writes (based on the *Acharonim* mentioned) that *lechatchila* (ideally) one should eat two *kezayit* portions.[7]

---

6. According to Rashi, one must recline, as this is the obligatory *kezayit* of matza for which one must recline. However, the Rambam (*Hilchot Chametz Umatza* 7:8) holds that reclining is not necessary. Regarding this issue, the *Shulchan Aruch* rules that reclining is necessary. Another possible ramification is whether one may speak unnecessary words from the time of *motzee-matza* until after the eating of the *afikoman*: According to Rashi, perhaps one should not speak during this time so as not to interrupt between the *beracha* on the matza and the *afikoman*. This is in fact the opinion of the *Shelah* (beginning of *Masechet Pesachim*), though the *Shulchan Aruch* (475:1) indicates that this is not required. In addition, according to Rashi, one would presumably need to have the *afikoman* in mind when reciting the *beracha* of *al achilat matza*, as opposed to the two other opinions.

7. According to the *Chazon Ovadia*, the strict *halacha* is that only one *kezayit* is required, but who is stringent is praiseworthy.

33. שולחן ערוך | או"ח תעז:א

Shulchan Aruch, Orach Chaim 477:1

After the completion of the meal, each person eats a *kezayit* from the matza that has been concealed under the cloth, as a remembrance for the *korban pesach* that was eaten while sated.

לאחר גמר כל הסעודה אוכלים ממצה השמורה תחת המפה כזית כל אחד, זכר לפסח הנאכל על השובע.

34. משנה ברורה | תעז:א

Mishna Berura 477:1

Kezayit – *Lechatchila* one should take two *kezayit* portions, one as a remembrance for the *pesach*, and one as a remembrance for the matza that was eaten with it.

כזית – ולכתחילה טוב שיקח שני זיתים אחד זכר לפסח ואחד זכר למצה הנאכלת עמו.

The Time for Eating the *Afikoman*

The Gemara cites a Tannaitic dispute whether one must eat the *korban pesach* before *chatzot* (halachic midnight) or whether it is permitted to eat it until *alot hashachar* (dawn).

35. מסכת ברכות ט.

Masechet Berachot 9a

As it was taught in a *beraita*: **"And they shall eat of the meat on that night"** (*Shemot* 12:8); **Rabbi Elazar ben Azarya says: Here it is stated: "On that night,"** and the same expression **is stated below** in the same chapter: **"And I will pass through the land of Egypt on that night** and I will strike every firstborn in the land of Egypt, from person to animal" (*Shemot* 12:12). Therefore, **just as** in the verse **below,** the striking of the first-borns took place **until midnight,** as stated explicitly in the verse, **so too** in the verse **here,** the mitzva to eat the Paschal offering continues **until midnight.**

Rabbi Akiva said to him: Was it not already said, "Thus you shall eat it…**in haste [chipazon]**…" (*Shemot* 12:11)? Therefore the Paschal offering may be eaten **until the time of haste…** However, **with regard to what did they disagree? With regard to the time of haste. Rabbi Elazar ben Azarya held: What is the** meaning of **haste?** It is **the haste of the Egyptians** at midnight, as they hurried to the houses of the people of Israel to send them away, in fear of the plague of the firstborn.

דתניא: "ואכלו את הבשר בלילה הזה", רבי אלעזר בן עזריה אומר: נאמר כאן בלילה הזה ונאמר להלן ועברתי בארץ מצרים בלילה הזה – מה להלן עד חצות, אף כאן עד חצות. אמר ליה רבי עקיבא: והלא כבר נאמר בחפזון – עד שעת חפזון... על מה נחלקו – על שעת חפזון; רבי אלעזר בן עזריה סבר: מאי חפזון – חפזון דמצרים, ורבי עקיבא סבר: מאי חפזון – חפזון דישראל. תניא נמי הכי: הוציאך ה' אלהיך ממצרים לילה – וכי בלילה יצאו? והלא לא יצאו אלא ביום, שנאמר: ממחרת הפסח יצאו בני ישראל ביד רמה! אלא: מלמד שהתחילה להם גאולה מבערב.

And Rabbi Akiva held: What is the meaning of **haste?** It is **the haste of Israel** in the morning, as they rushed to leave Egypt. **It was also taught** in a *beraita*: **"The Lord, your God, took you out from Egypt at night,"** but the question arises: **Did they leave at night? Didn't they leave during the day, as it is stated: "On the day after** the offering of the **Paschal** offering, **the children of Israel went out with a high hand"? Rather, this teaches that the redemption began for them in the evening.**

🕎 Rashi, Berachot 9a | רש"י | ברכות ט. 36.

The haste of the Egyptians – Referring to the plague of the firstborn, for through it they hastened to send them away.

חפזון דמצרים – מכת הבכורים, שעל ידם נחפזו למהר לשלחם.

The haste of Israel – They didn't listen to them [the Egyptians] to leave until the morning.

חפזון דישראל – לא שמעו להם לצאת עד בקר.

According to the Gemara, both Rabbi Elazar ben Azaryah and Rabbi Akiva agree that the *korban pesach* must be eaten during the time of *chipazon*, haste, since it says they must eat in haste. The former though argues that it must be eaten during the time when the Egyptians were in haste, i.e., at night when they hastened them away, while the latter claims the haste was that of the Jews, who did not actually leave until the morning. Therefore, the *korban pesach* may be eaten until dawn.

The *Rishonim* dispute in accordance with which opinion to rule. **Tosafot** (*Megilla* 21 s.v *lituyei*) and the **Mordechai** (*Berachot* ibid.), among others, rule in accordance with Rabbi Elazar Ben Azaryah that the *korban pesach* must be eaten by midnight. By contrast, the **Rambam** (*Hilchot Korban Pesach* 8:15) rules in accordance with the opinion of Rabbi Akiva. The ***Shulchan Aruch*** rules in the following manner:

Shulchan Aruch, Orach Chaim 477:1 | שולחן ערוך | או"ח תעז:א 37.

…One should be careful to eat it before *chatzot*…

...יהא זהיר לאכלו קודם חצות...

The language of "one should be careful" seems to indicate that strictly speaking, it is permitted to eat the *afikoman* after *chatzot* (in accordance with the opinion of Rabbi Akiva), but ideally one should eat it before *chatzot* (to be stringent for the opinion of Rabbi Elazar ben Azarya). The **Gra** also writes that one should finish eating the *afikoman* before *chatzot*, as does the **Mishna Berura**. However, the *Mishna Berura* indicates that if one did not do so, one should eat it afterwards.[8] This ruling is given even more explicitly by the ***Yalkut Yosef***:

✿ Yalkut Yosef, Moadim, Hilchot Pesach, Tzafun | ילקוט יוסף | מועדים, הל' פסח, צפון 38.

One should be careful to eat the *afikoman* before *chatzot*, but *bedieved*, one fulfills one's obligation even after *chatzot*.

יזהר לאכול האפיקומן קודם חצות, ובדיעבד יוצא ידי חובה גם לאחר חצות.

---

8. The Responsa *Avnei Nezer* (o.c. 381) suggests a novel solution for one who realizes that he will not finish his meal and eat the *afikoman* before midnight: Just before midnight he should eat a *kezayit* of matza and stipulate the following condition – if the *halacha* is in accordance with the opinion of Rabbi Elazar Ben Azarya, then this *kezayit* will be his *afikoman*, and if the *halacha* follows Rabbi Akiva, then it is considered to be a regular act of eating matza. After this, he should not eat anything until after midnight. After midnight, he may continue eating his meal in any event; for if the *halacha* is like Rabbi Elazar Ben Azarya, the prohibition to eat is only in effect until midnight (when in his view the mitzva of eating the *afikoman* has already terminated) if the *halacha* is in accordance with Rabbi Akiva, then it is permitted to continue eating and complete the *afikoman* until *alot hashachar*. We should note that this novelty is based on a number of assumptions, many of which are debatable, but an elaboration of the issue is beyond the scope of this *shiur*.

Which Drinks Are Prohibited Following the *Afikoman*?

It is clear that the prohibition to eat following the *afikoman* mentioned above includes all solid foods. With regard to liquids, the **Shulchan Aruch** and **Rema** indicate that all drinks are prohibited except for water (and the final two cups of wine).

| **Shulchan Aruch, Orach Chaim 481:1** | **39. שולחן ערוך | או"ח תפא:א** |

After the four cups, one is not permitted to drink wine; only water. **Rema**: And all [other] drinks have the status of wine.

אחר ארבע כוסות אינו רשאי לשתות יין
אלא מים.
הגה: וכל המשקין דינם כיין.

Nevertheless, the **Mishna Berura** notes that drinks that do not have a strong taste and do not remove the taste of the matza from one's mouth are permitted to drink. Based on that, *poskim* discuss whether one may drink tea or coffee after the *afikoman*.

| **Piskei Teshuvot 481:1** | **40. פסקי תשובות | תפא:א** |

Coffee and tea without sugar, seltzer and water are permitted even *lechatchila* (though coffee and tea with sugar remove the taste of the matza), and some [*Rishonim*] are stringent [against the *Shulchan Aruch*] even regarding drinking water, and certainly concerning coffee and tea… the prohibition of eating and drinking takes effect from the conclusion of the consumption of the *afikoman*… and the prohibitions remains until dawn.

קפה ותה בלי סוכר, סודה ומים מותר אף
לכתחילה (אבל קפה ותה עם סוכר מבטל
טעם מצה), ויש שהחמירו אף בשתיית מים
וכל שכן קפה ותה... שאיסור אכילה ושתיה
חל מגמר אכילת האפיקומן... ואיסורו הוא
עד עלות השחר.

According to the **Piskei Teshuvot**, it is permitted to drink coffee and tea without sugar since these drinks do not dispel the taste of the matza, though drinking them with sugar would not be allowed. The **Yalkut Yosef** goes one step further and allows drinking them even with sugar when one is trying to stay awake in order to study the *halachot* of the Seder or the story of *yetziat mitzrayim*. In addition, he states that one may be more lenient after *chatzot* (as opposed to the *Piskei Teshuvot* who rules that are prohibited apply until dawn), since some rule that the restrictions upon eating do not apply after *chatzot*.

| **Yalkut Yosef, Moadim, Hilchot Pesach, Tzafun** | **41. ילקוט יוסף | מועדים, הל' פסח, צפון** |

It is permitted to drink water after the *afikoman*, but not wine other than the two cups that the Sages instituted. One who is sitting and learning the laws of Pesach and the story of the Exodus after Hallel and the fourth cup is permitted to drink tea or coffee (even with sugar) in order to keep oneself awake and dispel [the effects] of the wine. However, one should not be lenient without a need. After midnight there is more room to be lenient.

מותר לשתות מים אחר האפיקומן, אבל
לא יין חוץ משתי כוסות שתקנו חז"ל.
והיושב ועוסק בהלכות פסח ובסיפור יציאת
מצרים אחר ההלל, וכוס רביעית, רשאי
לשתות קפה או תה, (ואפילו עם סוכר),
כדי להתעורר ולהפיג יינו. אבל בלא צורך
אין להקל, ולאחר חצות יש להקל בזה יותר.

BARECH

At first glance, it seems that the laws of *Birkat Hamazon* (Grace after Meals) on the Seder night are no different than those of *Birkat Hamazon* during the rest of the year. Nevertheless there are a few minor differences between them mentioned by the *poskim* cited below.

Zimun

The **Shulchan Aruch** rules that one should try to ensure that *Birkat Hamazon* is recited with a *zimun* (special introduction recited when there are three individuals). The **Mishna Berura** explains that the reason for this is to ensure that *Hallel* is recited with at least three people.

| א | Shulchan Aruch, Orach Chaim 479:1 | 42. שולחן ערוך \| או"ח תעט:א |

There is a mitzva to ensure one has a *zimun*.

מצוה לחזור אחר זימון.

| א | Mishna Berura 479:9 | 43. משנה ברורה \| תעט:ט |

The *Acharonim* agree that the *zimun* is not for the purpose of *Birkat Hamazon*, for there is no obligation to enhance [the mitzva] more than the rest of the year for this reason. Here it is for the *Hallel*, as there is a mitzva of enhancement to recite *Hallel* with [at least] three.

הסכימו האחרונים דהאי זימון אינו לענין בהמ"ז דבשביל זה אינו מחוייב להדר יותר מבשאר ימות השנה והכא לענין הלל מיירי שמצוה להדר לומר הלל בשלשה.

Reciting *Birkat Hamazon* Over a Cup of Wine

The **Shulchan Aruch** (182:1) cites a number of opinions as to whether there is an obligation to recite *Birkat Hamazon* over a cup of wine. The **Mishna Berura** writes there that the custom is to be lenient unless wine is readily available, such as on Shabbat and Yom Tov, in which case it is ideal to do so over a cup of wine.

However, on the Seder night, there is an obligation to recite *Birkat Hamazon* over a cup of wine. Moreover, the common practice, as recorded in the **Shulchan Aruch** below, is that each individual recites the *Birkat Hamazon* over his own cup of wine and drinks it, as this is the third of the four cups. The basis for this practice seems to be the following comment of **Tosafot**:

🔖 **Tosafot, Pesachim 105b**

...Since *Birkat Hamazon* requires a cup [of wine only] with three [people making a *zimun*],[9] they instituted using a cup on Pesach for *Birkat Hamazon* even for an individual.

44. תוספות | פסחים קה:

...משום דברכת המזון טעונה כוס בג' תיקנו בפסח אפילו ביחיד כוס לברכת המזון.

א **Shulchan Aruch, Orach Chaim 479:1**

After that, they pour him the third cup. He recites *Birkat Hamazon* and *borei pri hagafen* (the blessing on the wine) upon it.

45. שולחן ערוך | או"ח תעט:א

אחר כך מוזגין לו כוס שלישי, ומברך עליו ברכת המזון ובורא פרי הגפן.

The **Mishna Berura** explains the reason for this practice is that it is appropriate to use each of the four cups for a different mitzva.

א **Mishna Berura 479:2**

Even if one recites [*Birkat Hamazon*] by oneself, and even according to the opinion that *Birkat Hamazon* does not require [the use of] a cup, nevertheless since the Sages instituted to drink four cups of wine on this night, it is appropriate to perform a mitzva with each cup. Therefore, we connect the third cup with *Birkat Hamazon*.

46. משנה ברורה | תעט:ב

אפילו אם מברך ביחידי ואפילו למ"ד בעלמא דבהמ"ז אינה טעונה כוס מ"מ הואיל שתקנו חכמים לשתות ארבעה כוסות בלילה זו יש לעשות מצוה בכל כוס וכוס להכי סומכין כוס שלישי לבהמ"ז.

One Who Forgot to Recite *Ya'aleh Veyavo*

One who forgot to recite *Ya'aleh Veyavo* (the addition recited on Rosh Chodesh and festivals) in *Birkat Hamazon* must recite *Birkat Hamazon* again from the beginning. This is the halacha according to all opinions, as whenever there is an obligation to eat bread, one must repeat *Birkat Hamazon* if *Ya'aleh Veyavo* was forgotten, and there is clearly an obligation to eat a *kezayit* of matza on the Seder night. In addition, **Rabbi Akiva Eiger** writes that this is true even with regard to women, despite the fact that on other days of Yom Tov she may not be required to repeat it.

א **Responsa of Rabbi Akiva Eiger, Mahadura Kamma, Siman 1**

Regarding the people of his household who forgot to mention the festival [i.e., *Ya'aleh Veyavo*] in *Birkat Hamazon*... after all this, if I were asked regarding the matter, I think I would rule that all men of his household should repeat *Birkat Hamazon* but not the women and girls.

47. שו"ת רבי עקיבא איגר | מהדורא קמא, סימן א

על אודות בני ביתו ששכחו להזכיר של חג בברכת המזון... ועכ"ז אלו נשאלתי אנכי על ככה, כמדומה הייתי מורה ובא, דכל מרבית ביתו אנשים יחזרו לברך, אבל לא הנשים והבנות.

---

9. Although as noted above, the common practice today does not always follow this opinion that one must use a cup of wine when reciting *Birkat Hamazon* with a *zimun*, Tosafot can still be used as a basis for the notion that an additional obligation was added that each individual drink the cup on Pesach night. [Addition of the English editors]

My reasoning is that I can argue that women are permitted to fast on Yom Tov, as the prohibition to fast on Yom Tov appears to be is rooted in the obligation of *oneg* (enjoying it through eating and drinking) as the Rambam states. And the mitzva of *oneg* is included in the positive mitzva of "it shall be a festival for you," and we extrapolate from that half should be for Hashem and half for yourselves. **If so, this mitzva should not be better than any other positive time-bound mitzva, from which women are exempt, excluding the first night of Pesach, where they are obligated to [eat] matza based on the comparison** [in the Gemara, *Pesachim* 5a] **that whoever is forbidden to eat chametz is obligated to eat matza.**

וטעמא דידי משום דיש לי לדון דאשה מותרת להתענות בי"ט, דאיסור תענית בי"ט נראה שהוא מדין עונג, וכן הוא ברמב"ם, והרי מצות עונג הוא בכלל מצות עשה דעצרת תהיה לכם, דדרשינן מניה חציו לד' וחציו לכם, וא"כ לא תהא מצוה זו עדיפא מכל מ"ע שהזמן גרמא שנשים פטורות, זולת בליל א' דפסח דמחוייבות במצה מהקישא דכל שישנו בבל תאכל חמץ.

Rabbi Akiva Eiger here explains that women are obligated to eat matza based on a comparison made by the Torah (*Shemot* 12:19–20) between the prohibition of eating chametz and the positive mitzva of eating matza. Just as a woman is subject to the former, so too she is included in the latter. Since the general rule is that one must repeat *Birkat Hamazon* when forgetting *Ya'aleh Veyavo* after any meal that one was obligated to eat, therefore even women must repeat *Birkat Hamazon* on the Seder night, when they are obligated to consume matza like men.

HALLEL

The **Mishna** states that they used to recite *Hallel* while eating the *korban pesach,* and the **Gemara** cites the source for this.

Masechet Pesachim 95a

MISHNA: What is the difference **between** the Paschal offering offered on **the first** *Pesach* and the Paschal offering offered on **the second** *Pesach* [Pesach Sheni, on the 14th of Iyyar]? On **the first it is prohibited** to own leavened bread due to the prohibitions: **It shall not be seen, and: It shall not be found. And** on **the second** *Pesach* it is permissible for one to have both **leavened bread and** *matza* with him in the house. **The first** *Pesach* **requires** the recitation of *Hallel* **as it is eaten and the second does not require** the recitation of *Hallel* **as it is eaten.**

GEMARA: From where are these matters derived that one must recite *Hallel* while eating the Paschal offering on the first *Pesach*?

Rabbi Yochanan said, citing Rabbi Shimon ben Yehotzadak, that **the verse states: "You shall have a song as in the night when a Festival is sanctified"** (*Yeshayahu* 30:29). From here it may be derived that **a night sanctified as a Festival,** on which labor is prohibited, such as the first night of Passover, **requires** the recitation of *Hallel*; however, **a night that is not sanctified as a Festival,** such as the night when the Paschal offering is eaten following the second *Pesach*, **does not require** the recitation of *Hallel.*

48. מסכת פסחים צה.

משנה: מה בין פסח הראשון לשני? הראשון אסור בבל יראה ובל ימצא והשני חמץ ומצה עמו בבית. הראשון טעון הלל באכילתו והשני אינו טעון הלל באכילתו.

גמרא: מנא הני מילי? אמר רבי יוחנן משום רבי שמעון בן יהוצדק: אמר קרא – "השיר יהיה לכם כליל התקדש חג" – לילה המקודש לחג טעון הלל, לילה שאין מקודש לחג אין טעון הלל.

There are a number of distinctions between *Hallel* recited on the Seder night and *Hallel* recited at other times.

- **Reciting a *beracha* over *Hallel***

At other times when the entire *Hallel* is recited, there is an accompanying *beracha* recited beforehand, but at the Seder, we do not recite a *beracha*.

- **The obligation of women**

Women are generally exempt from saying *Hallel* since it is a time-bound mitzva, but on the Seder night, they too are obligated to recite *Hallel*. **Tosafot** explain the reason for the difference.

Tosafot, Sukkah 38a

Who was a slave and a woman – It is evident from here that a woman is exempt from [reciting] *Hallel* of Sukkot and similarly for Shavuot. And the reason is that it is a time-bound mitzva. Even though regarding *Hallel* on the night of Pesach it appears from chapter *Arvei Pesachim* (108a) that she is obligated in the four cups and presumably they instituted the four cups only in order to recite *Hallel* and the *Haggada* on them, *Hallel* of Pesach

49. תוספות | סוכה לח.

שהיה עבד ואשה – משמע כאן דאשה פטורה מהלל דסוכות וכן דעצרת וטעמא משום דמצוה שהזמן גרמא היא אף על גב דבהלל דלילי פסחים משמע בפרק ערבי פסחים (דף קח.) דמחייבי בד' כוסות ומסתמא לא תיקנו ד' כוסות אלא כדי לומר

is different, as it commemorates a miracle, and they [women] too were part of the miracle. But here it is not recited for the miracle [but rather for the holiday itself].

עליהם הלל ואגדה שאני הלל דפסח דעל הנס בא ואף הן היו באותו הנס אבל כאן לא על הנס אמור.

Tosafot here invoke the principle of *af hein hayu b'oto haneis*, "they were also included in the miracle," which is used elsewhere in the Gemara to explain why women are obligated in certain specific time-bound mitzvot, such as reading the *megilla* on Purim. Here, too, Tosafot explain that since women were also redeemed from Egypt, they also have an obligation to recite *Hallel*, despite its status as a time-bound mitzva.

Hallel at Night

Hallel is generally recited during the day, as is clarified by the Mishna in *Megilla*.

⦿ Masechet Megilla 20b   50. מסכת מגילה כ:

The entire day is valid for the reading of the *megilla* and reciting of *Hallel*… this is the general rule: Any matter where the mitzva is during the day, it is valid the entire day…

היום כשר לקריאת המגילה ולקריאת ההלל... זה הכלל: דבר שמצותו ביום כשר כל היום...

If so, why do we recite *Hallel* at the Seder? This question was dealt with by the **Chatam Sofer**.

א Responsa Chatam Sofer 1:51   51. שו"ת חתם סופר | א:נא

But we need to answer regarding *Hallel* on the night of Pesach, for the fact that we recite it sitting down has already been addressed by the *Beit Yosef* at the end of *siman* 422, but if we say that night is not the [appropriate] time for *Hallel*, if so one may ask from the night of Pesach [where *Hallel* is recited]? And one must answer that specifically *Hallel* that we recite on every festival and day of redemption where the Sages instituted to recite it when they are redeemed, as is brought in *Pesachim* 117a, regarding these we apply [the verse] "from when the sun rises in the east until it comes," and not at night, for this is how they established it. **But regarding Seder night, which is the actual time of the miracle, about this it was stated "the song will be for you on the night of the sanctification of the Festival."**

אלא דצריך יישוב הלל דליל פסח, דמה שאומרים מיושב כבר כ' ב"י ססי' תכ"ב אבל אי נימא דלילה לאו זמן הלל הוא א"כ תיקשי מליל פסח וצ"ל דוקא הלל שקורין בכל יום טוב ויום גאולה שתיקנו לומר לכשיגאלו כדאיתא בפסחים קי"ז ע"א בהאי אמרינן ממזרח שמש עד מבואו ולא בלילה כי כך תיקנו, **אבל בליל פסח שהיא שעת הנס ממש על זה נאמר השיר יהי' לכם כליל התקדש חג.**

According to the *Chatam Sofer*, *Hallel* at the Seder is unique because it is recited at the actual time that the miracle occurred, as this is when the Egyptian first-born were killed, and when they prepared to depart from Egypt. For this reason, the verse quoted that discusses singing at night can be applied to permit reciting *Hallel* at night.

It seems that the basis for these three distinctions between *Hallel* recited on Pesach night and *Hallel* recited at other times is that the essential nature of the two is different. The standard *Hallel* serves to thank Hashem for past events, whereas *Hallel* at the Seder is a song of thanksgiving for the *present,* as were our forefathers not redeemed, we would still be enslaved, plus we are supposed to feel as if we ourselves have departed Egypt, as is stated in the *Haggada*. This distinction appears to be explicit in the words of **Rav Hai Gaon** quoted in the **Ran** below.

 Ran, Pesachim 26b in the Pagination of the Rif

52. ר"ן | פסחים כו: בדפי הרי"ף

But Rabbeinu Hai Gaon *z"l* wrote in a responsum that we don't recite the blessing of "to complete the *Hallel*,"[10] for we don't recite it as something one reads, but rather as one singing a song.

אבל רבינו האי גאון ז"ל כתב בתשובה שאין מברכין על הלל שבלילי פסחים לגמור את ההלל שאין אנו קוראין אותו בתורת קורין אלא בתורת אומר שירה.

In other words, no *beracha*[11] is recited here because the Sages did not institute an enactment to *recite* the *Hallel*, but rather it should be a spontaneous song that we should burst out singing in gratitude to Hashem for being redeemed from slavery for the merit of being His servants. By contrast, *Hallel* recited on other days, such as Chanukah, is primarily designed to thank Hashem for past miracles performed for our forefathers.

This also explains why women are obligated in reciting this *Hallel*. Since they were also part of the miracle, and the *Hallel* is recited to thank Hashem for the feeling of redemption, women certainly have as much reason to praise Hashem as do men.

---

10. This is the formulation used today by Sephardic Jews on days when the complete *Hallel* is recited (in Hebrew: *ligmor et haHallel*). The common formulation for this *beracha* used by Ashkenazic Jews, though, is "to read the *Hallel* (*likro et haHallel*)." [Addition of the English editors]

11. Similarly, it is understandable according to this why we recite the *Hallel* sitting down at the *Seder*, as opposed to other times when we recite *Hallel*, for here it is the *Hallel* of song, and not simply the fulfillment of the rabbinic enactment to recite *Hallel* (which must be said while standing).

NIRTZA

We complete the *Hallel* section of the Seder by drinking the fourth and final cup and reciting a *beracha acharona* (after-blessing) on the wine. At that point, the final section of the Seder begins, known as *Nirtza*, when we ask Hashem to find favor [*nirtza*] with our Seder ceremony. We pray that just as Hashem took us out of Egypt, so too will He take us out of this exile we can celebrate the Seder with the *korban pesach* very soon, and conclude by singing *leshana haba'ah biYerushalayim hebenuyah*, next year in rebuilt Jerusalem![12]

---

12. It should be noted that the songs found at the end of the *Haggada*, such as *Adir Hu* and *Chad Gadya* appear to be a later edition to the Seder, and were not found in the text of the *Haggada* of the *Rishonim*. [Addition of the English editors]

SUMMARY OF HALACHOT OF THE
SEDER NIGHT II

Maror

---

1. **Gemara/Rambam** – The mitzva of *maror* today applies by rabbinic law only.

2. **Which species should be used for *maror*?**

   a. **Gemara/*Shulchan Aruch*** – Romaine lettuce is the preferred choice.

   b. ***Chazon Ish*** – Regular lettuce that does not taste bitter should not be used.

   c. ***Yerushalmi/Shulchan Aruch HaRav*** – Lettuce is acceptable since it eventually becomes bitter, even if it is not bitter when consumed. The key factor is that it is defined as a species of *maror*.

   d. ***Minchat Asher*** – Agrees that non-bitter *maror* may be used, the key is it must be eaten in a way that the bitterness can be tasted if it does contain some.

3. **How to eat the *maror***

   a. ***Yere'im*** – One must eat a *kezayit,* the standard definition of eating.

   b. **Gemara/*Shulchan Aruch*** – One does not recline when eating the *maror*.

   c. ***Shulchan Aruch/Mishna Berura*** – One dips the *maror* into *charoset* to remove the harmful elements and then shakes off some of the *charoset*.

   d. No *beracha* on vegetables is recited on the *maror*.

      i. **Tosafot** – The reason is that it is included in foods that are eaten as part of a meal.

      ii. **Rosh** – The *beracha* on the *Karpas* already exempted it.

Korech

---

1. **Gemara** – Hillel and Chachamim dispute whether to eat the matza and *maror* separately or together. The dispute is not resolved, so we first eat them separately and then both together.

2. ***Shulchan Aruch*** – Rules like the conclusion of the Gemara, and that for *Korech* we must eat a *kezayit* of matza and *maror* while reclining.

Shulchan Orech

1. **Mishna/Shulchan Aruch** – The custom in some places is not to eat roast meat on the Seder night, while in others it is eaten.

2. *Mishna Berura* – The custom today is not to do so, and pot roast, as well as roast that was cooked first, are included in the custom.

3. **Rema** – The custom is to eat eggs either to commemorate the *korban pesach* that we no longer bring or as a sign of mourning since Tisha B'av falls out on the same night of the week.

4. **Gra** – We do not express mourning on a *Yom Tov*; eating eggs commemorates the *korban chagiga*.

5. **Rema** – One should not eat or drink too much at the meal to ensure that the *afikoman* is eaten with an appetite and that one does not fall asleep from excessive food or wine.

Tzafun

1. **Mishna/Gemara** – One may not eat any dessert [*afikoman*] following the consumption of the *korban pesach*.

2. **Gemara** – One also may not eat any dessert [*afikoman*] following the consumption of matza for *Tzafun*.

3. **Why do we eat the *Afikoman*?**
   a. **Rashi** – This is the fulfillment of the biblical mitzva of eating matza.
   b. **Rosh** – It serves as a commemoration for the *korban pesach*.
   c. **Tosafot** – So that the taste of matza will remain in one's mouth at the end of the Seder.

4. **How much *matza* must one eat?**
   a. *Bach* – Two *kezayit* portions, one for the *korban pesach* and one for the matza eaten with the *pesach*.
   b. *Shulchan Aruch* – One *kezayit* for the *korban pesach*.
   c. *Mishna Berura* – Ideally one should eat 2 *kezayit* portions.

5. **The proper time for eating the *Afikoman***
   a. **Gemara** – It is a dispute:
      i. **Rabbi Elazar ben Azarya** – Until *chatzot*.
      ii. **Rabbi Akiva** – Until dawn.

   b. **Shulchan Aruch/Gra/Mishna Berura** – One should be careful to eat it before *chatzot*.

   c. **Mishna Berura/Yalkut Yosef** – *Bedieved*, one may eat it after *chatzot* as well.

6. **Drinking after the Afikoman**

   a. **Shulchan Aruch** – One may not drink any drinks except for water.

   b. **Mishna Berura** – Drinks that do not have a strong taste are permitted.

   c. **Piskei Teshuvot** – Tea or coffee without sugar are permitted.

   d. **Yalkut Yosef** – Even tea or coffee with sugar are permitted if being used to help one continue discussing the story of *yetziat mitzrayim* or the *halachot* of Pesach.

Barech

1. **Making a zimun**

   a. **Shulchan Aruch** – One should try to have enough people at the Seder to make a *zimun*.

   b. **Mishna Berura** – This is in order to have at least three people reciting *Hallel* together, which is preferable.

2. **Using a cup of wine for Birkat Hamazon**

   a. **Tosafot** – Unlike other times of the year, at the Seder every person recites *Birkat Hamazon* on a cup of wine.

   b. **Shulchan Aruch** – Every person recites *Birkat Hamazon* on a cup of wine.

   c. **Mishna Berura** – Each of the four cups is used in conjunction with another mitzva.

3. **Forgetting Ya'aleh Veyavo**

   a. **Rabbi Akiva Eiger** – Both men and women must repeat *Birkat Hamazon* if it was forgotten, since both are obligated to eat a *kezayit* of matza.

Hallel

1. **Gemara** – One recites *Hallel* together with the consumption of the *korban pesach*.

2. **Differences between Hallel at the Seder and Hallel recited at other times**

   a. There is no *beracha* recited at the Seder.

   b. Women generally are exempt from reciting *Hallel*.

   c. *Hallel* is usually recited only during the day.

    i.   **Chatam Sofer** – *Hallel* is recited at night at the Seder because it is considered praise for a miracle that just happened now.

   ii.   **Ran** – *Hallel* at the Seder is not considered a standard recitation, but rather a spontaneous expression of song and praise for Hashem.

Nirtza

1.   We declare "next year in Jerusalem" after drinking the fourth cup and reciting a *beracha acharona.*

2.   This is when we ask Hashem to find favor with our Seder experience and bring us the final redemption speedily.

Made in the USA
Coppell, TX
04 April 2022

75965559R10072